INSTRUMENT REPAIR
FOR THE MUSIC TEACHER

by Burton Stanley

Photos by
Rick Washik
Potsdam, New York

16380 Roscoe Blvd., Suite 200,
Van Nuys, CA 91406

Printed and bound in the United States of America

Library of Congress Cataloging in Publication Data

Stanley, Burton.
Instrument repair for the music teacher.

Includes index.
1. Musical instruments–Repairing. I. Title.
ML460.S76 788'.05'2028 78-11832
ISBN 0-88284-075-4

INSTRUMENT REPAIR

FOR THE MUSIC TEACHER

by Burton Stanley

CONTENTS

1
NECESSARY EQUIPMENT

Certain aspects of repair and preventive maintenance of band instruments can be accomplished by the instrumental teacher with considerable benefit to the pupils, the program and the school system.

This means some additional effort is necessary on the part of the teacher, but the time and money saved will make it very worth while. Often an instrument is held for several weeks in a shop waiting its turn for a minor repair that could have been made in a few minutes at school. The time saved could mean the difference between success and failure in terms of pupil interest and accomplishment.

No one expects or asks you to become a repair technician. At considerable expense, you have spent a lifetime to date practicing and studying to become a teacher. The point is that with but little additional effort you can make your teaching many times more effective. Your pupils are your prime concern. Give them this additional advantage.

Some equipment is necessary. The following lists should be helpful in getting started. After a year of experimenting you will have a fairly good idea of what repairs you want to make and the equipment needed to do the job. Most schools are willing to invest a nominal sum of money in materials when the teacher gives of his time and skill to effect the repair. Making even the most minor repairs will substantially reduce your repair budget.

In order to submit an accurate requisition, you should send for catalogs from the following three major suppliers of instrument repair materials:

Ferree's Band Instrument Tools and Supplies
1477 E. Michigan
Battle Creek, Michigan 49016

Ed Myers Co. Band Instrument Repair Supplies
1622 Webster Street
Omaha, Nebraska 68102

MINIMUM ESSENTIAL TOOLS

alcohol lamp
triangular scraper
regular pliers
smooth jaw pliers
wire cutting pliers
round nose pliers
screwdriver —
  about 1/16-inch blade width
screwdriver —
  about 3/32-inch blade width

(list continued on pg. 4)

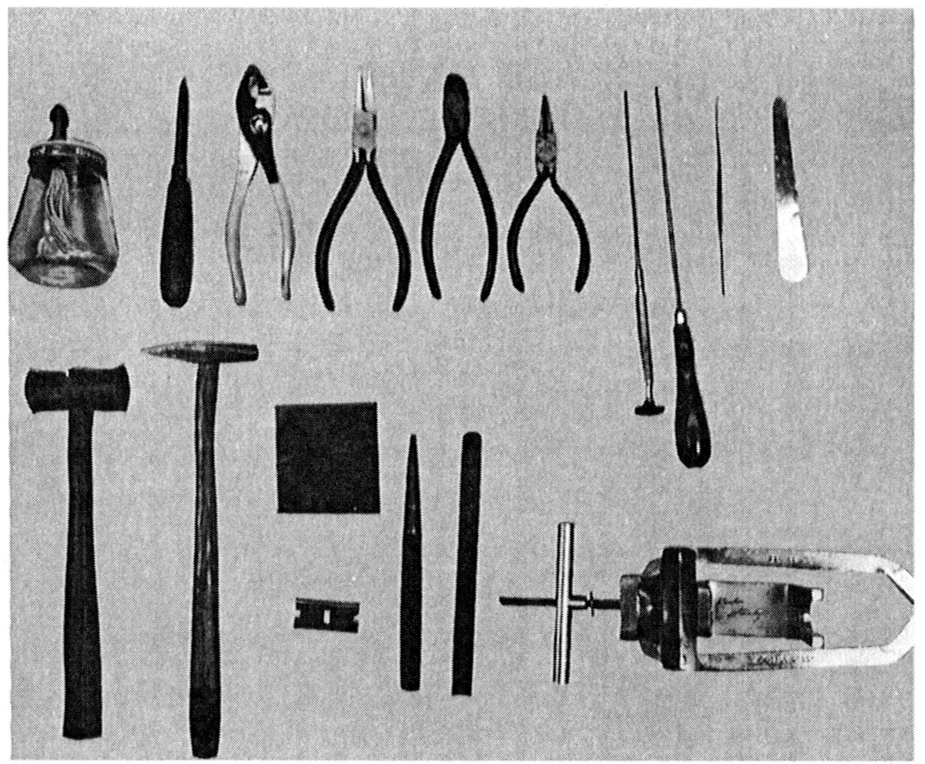

Photo 1. Minimum Essential Tools

Top row, left to right: alcohol lamp, triangular scraper, regular pliers, smooth jaw pliers, wire cutting pliers, round nose pliers, screwdriver–about 1/16-inch blade width, screwdriver–about 3/32-inch blade width, spring hook, pad slick.

Bottom row, left to right: rawhide mallet, bench hammer, hardened bench anvil, single edge razor blade, tapered punch, 6-inch steel rule, mouthpiece puller.

MINIMUM ESSENTIAL TOOLS (Cont.)

spring hook
pad slick
rawhide mallet
bench hammer
hardened bench anvil
single edge razor blade
tapered punch
6-inch steel rule
mouthpiece puller

MINIMUM ESSENTIAL SUPPLIES

muriatic acid – one quart
wide mouth glass jar and
  cover for water and acid mixture
denatured alcohol or
  synthetic fuel for lamp
contact cement
"3-in-1" or any light
  electric motor oil
pad cement
penetrating oil
1 sheet 1/64-inch cork
2 sheets 1/32-inch cork
1 sheet 1/16-inch cork
assortment of:
  french horn corks (12)
  water key corks (100)
  cork valve washers (100)
  felt valve washers (100)
  beveled medium-thick
    clarinet pads (100)
  flute pads (100)
  needle springs (100)
  flat springs (100)

SUGGESTED ADDITIONAL SUPPLIES

clarinet pads (100 each)
  size: 9½mm, 10mm, 16½mm
flute pads (100 each)
  size: 17½mm, 18mm
assortment of pads (100)
  alto, bass clarinet and bassoon

Most commercial alcohol lamps have a loose fitting cover for the wick or no cover at all. Consequently the fuel evaporates very rapidly. With but little effort you can make a lamp that remedies this situation. For the fuel reservoir use a small glass jar that has a metal screw top with a bonded rubber gasket. At a hardware store or an electrical supply house buy a 3/8-inch outside diameter brass nipple two or three inches long threaded full length on the outside. Get two thin hex-nuts and a beehive shaped closed nut for the end that fit the nipple. This closed nut is the type that usually holds a glass globe to a ceiling fixture.

Drill a hole in the jar lid to fit the nipple. If your jar is more than an inch wide at the top, drill this hole off center so that the diameter of the lid will not be in your way as you hold a clarinet up to the side of the flame. The wick can be made of regular cotton grocery string folded over until it fills the inside diameter of the nipple, or use candle wicking if it is readily available. This type of lamp will greatly retard the evaporation of the fuel, and if you care to solder the nuts to the cover, or use rubber O-rings or cork gaskets on both top and bottom of the lid under the nuts, you can tip your lamp over for easy carrying in your tool kit. (Photo 2.)

If you have access to a power grinder or can get the shop teacher in your school to grind it for you, you can make an excellent triangular scraper from a worn out three cornered file. Break the file off about 3 inches from the tang. Drill a hole in the end of a piece of 1/2- or 5/8-inch dowel. Make the hole about as large as the center of the taper on the tang, and

Photo 2. Homemade Alcohol Lamp

then grind the sides of the file until all traces of the cutting diagonals are ground away. Bring the broken end to a curved point as seen in Photo 3. Putting a ferrule on the dowel, or wrapping it with wire before driving in the tang, will lessen the danger of the dowel splitting. The file will break off easily by putting it in a vise. Extend that part you wish broken off above the vise jaws and hit the protruding end a sharp blow with a hammer. Guard your eyes as the broken piece will fly. Grind your scraper to the shape shown in the photo. You will use this tool in many different ways, but you need it right now to clean the old cork from tenons that need recorking.

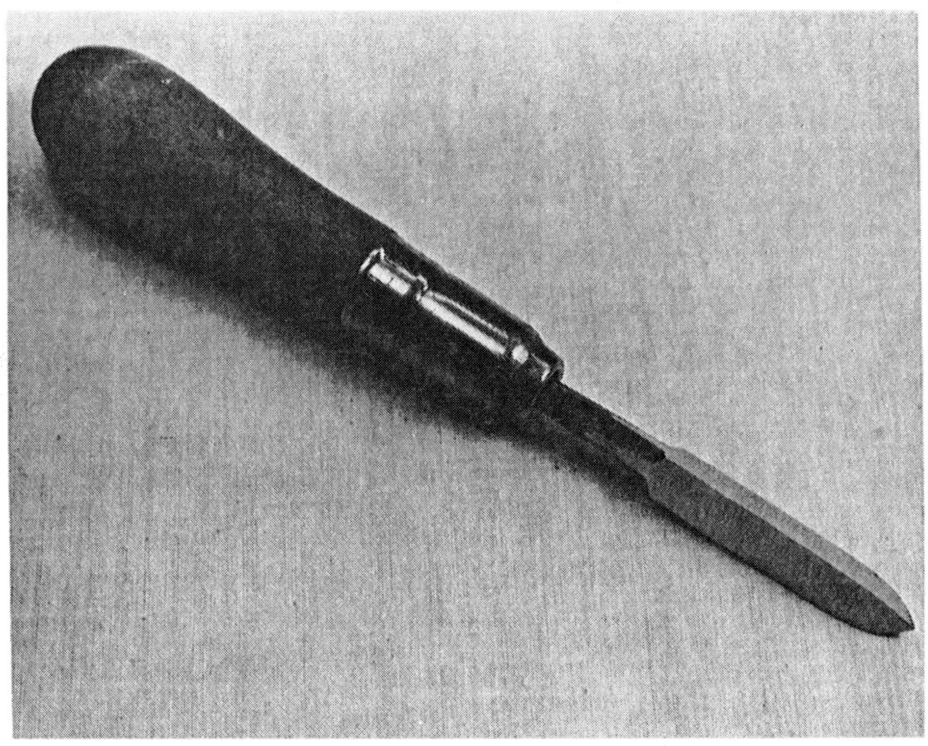

Photo 3. Homemade Scraper

An excellent spring hook can be made from a crochet hook if you make a few changes. File or grind a V-notch in the hook end. Taper handle end and notch. (See photos 4 and 5.) Many springs are easier to reach if you put a gentle curve in the hook. Buy a bigger hook for heavier sax springs.

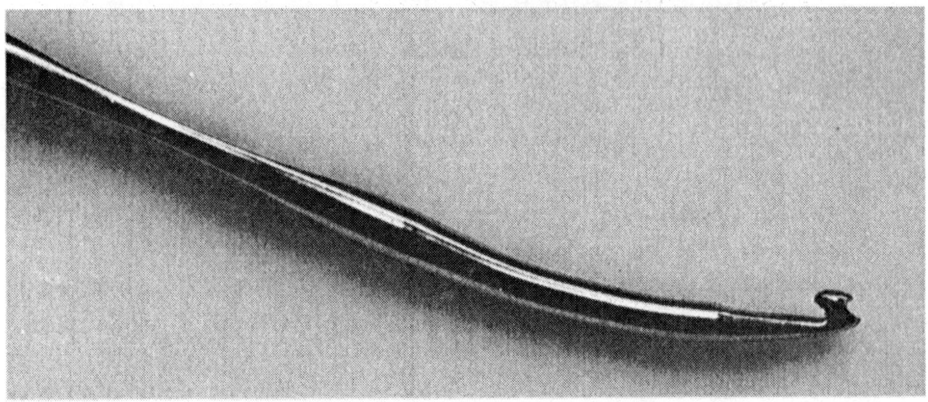

Photo 4. Homemade Spring Hook

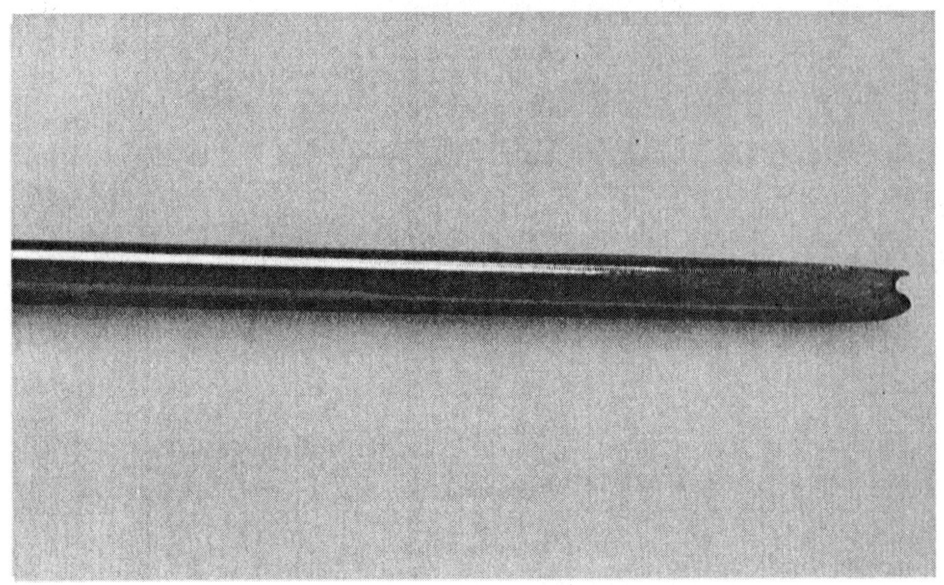

Photo 5. Homemade Spring Hook – Handle End

Again with the aid of your school shop teacher, a pad slick may be made from any piece of metal that is thin enough, but very strong and very springy. A nail file handle, a kitchen case knife blade or spatula, a putty knife, or a hack saw blade usually are the correct types of metal from which to make a pad slick. For clarinet one of the handiest slicks I have I ground from a hack saw blade to the shape shown in Photo 6. This would of course be too small for saxophone or the low clarinets. Make a larger one from a putty knife or kitchen spatula for larger pads.

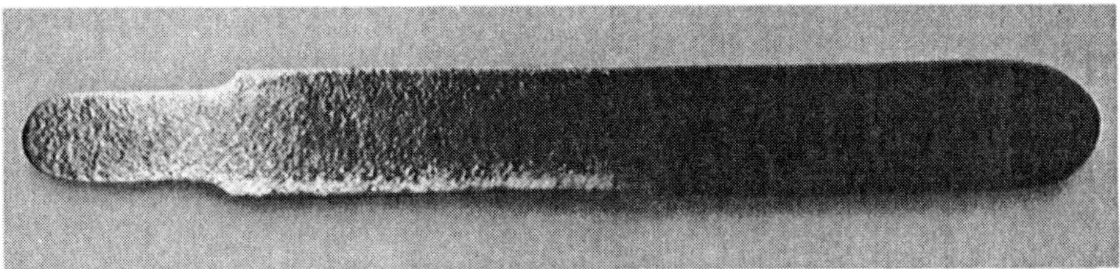

Photo 6. Pad Slick

Made from a hack saw blade. Actual size 4" long by ½" wide.

Make up a dozen or so feeler gauges by cutting strips of "Sight-Saver" eye glasses cleaning paper into strips about 1/4-inch wide and 1-inch long. Using "Duco" cement or pad cement, fasten one end of the paper strip to a light wooden handle such as half of a popsicle stick. The end result should look something like Photo 7.

Photo 7. Feeler Gauge

With the exception of these feeler guages it is cheaper to buy the tools I have described than it is to make them, if you value your time. Many people, however, derive a great deal of personal satisfaction from making useful things, and if care is taken we can often make a tool that serves our particular purpose to better advantage than the commercial counterpart.

2

WOODEN INSTRUMENT BODY CARE

Meticulous care of the bore of a woodwind instrument is of vital importance. It is sad, but true, that students with but few exceptions will care for their instruments as their teacher demands or neglects.

Experts fail to agree as to whether or not moisture from the breath is a primary cause for the cracking of wood instruments. There is, however, almost total agreement that any buildup of the deposit from saliva is detrimental to good tone production and intonation. Theoretically then, every instrument using the breath for tone production should be swabbed or rinsed and dried every time it is used. This is impossible on brass instruments, but it is possible and practical for most of the woodwinds. The material from which the instrument is made whether it be wood, metal, plastic, or rubber, is irrelevant. The important thing is that the bore should be swabbed dry and clean every time following its use.

In my opinion, the ideal swab for a Bb soprano clarinet is a piece of cloth about half the size of a man's handkerchief or about 6 inches wide and 12 inches long. An old cloth that has been laundered many times seems to be softer and more absorbent than new cloth. Tie a slip knot in the end of a piece of 30 to 50 pound test fish line that you have cut to about 20 inches in length. Slip the knot over a corner of the cloth, into which has been folded a BB shot or small bead or stone no larger than 1/8-inch in diameter. Fold only enough of the cloth over to cover the bead and still allow the slip knot to grab the cloth all around below the bead. Pull the knot tight. Use a small lead sinker as a weight on the other end of the line and cover it with cloth or tape.

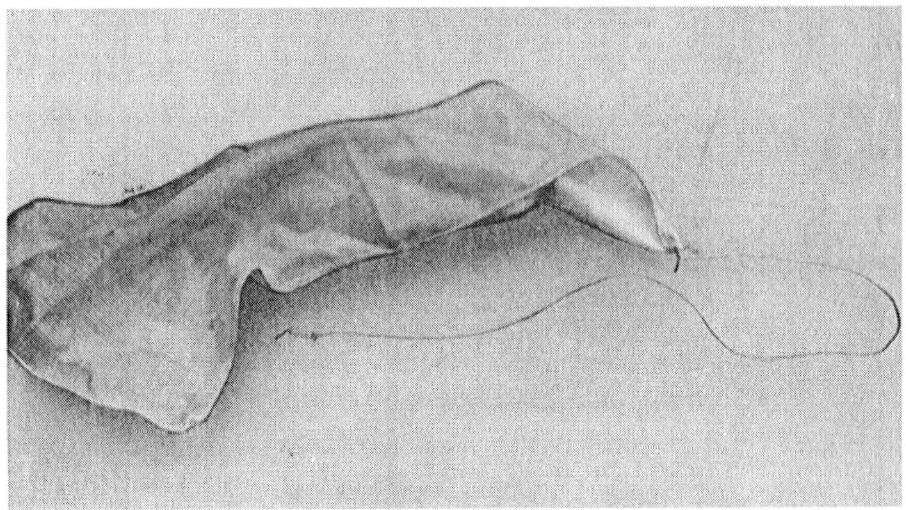

Photo 8. Homemade Clarinet Swab

Keep the clarinet assembled except for the mouthpiece and swab from the bell to the barrel at least twice, or until the bore is dry (Photo 9). Then take the instrument completely apart and dry any tenon socket that shows moisture, as shown in Photo 10. The mouthpiece should be wiped with a separate cloth.

Photo 9. Swabbing the Clarinet

Photo 10. Drying Wet Tenon Socket

There is a swab on the market using a tape-covered dowel with the tape sewn down the center of a triangular piece of cloth. This swab is very satisfactory. The principle advantage of the homemade one described is the ease with which the slip knot may be removed, allowing the cloth to be laundered. From a sanitary standpoint, the cloth should be exchanged for a clean one every week or two.

The most dangerous swab is the small chamois. Students tend to use this without completely unfolding it, and the resulting ball catches on the register key tube. Having but short length it cannot be pulled back out. Students try to push it out from the top, usually compacting the ball and tightening it within the bore. In removing a stuck swab of this type, remember it must be pulled back out and not pushed from the top. Use a long screwdriver, push it into the swab from the bottom, twisting the chamois around the edges of the screwdriver; pull slightly as you feel the material tighten around the screwdriver. A #8 wood screw with the head removed and brazed to a rod, as shown in Photo 11, works even better than the screwdriver. Ask your shop teacher or garage mechanic to make one for you.

Photo 11. Tool for Removing Stuck Swab

Bass and alto clarinets should be swabbed in the same manner using a cloth of a size in proportion to the bore. In addition to regular swabbing, the critical metal neck section should be washed with soap and water at least once a week using a sax neck brush. Remove the register key on those instruments that have one on the neck, because water will ruin the pad and rust the hinge. Remove the key from the bell and wash the bell at the same time to keep the bell bow clean.

The wooden Eb contra-bass clarinet must be carefully swabbed, but the metal BBb contra is so shaped that swabbing is impractical. Luckily most of the moisture is trapped in the removable neck section. This part of the instrument should be swabbed every time and washed frequently.

Care of the oboe bore is very controversial. Professional oboists have used a turkey feather for so many years it has become a custom. Actually, these feathers were originally placed on the bird to shed water and keep the bird dry and warm. They will absorb about as much moisture as a piece of tin. In response to my arguments, I am told that the feather is used not to remove the moisture, but as a brush to spread the moisture around in the bore. This, of course, does little to keep the very sensitive oboe bore free from saliva deposits. Oboe top joints crack with alarming regularity, and the oboists continue to spread the moisture around with the turkey feather. Clarinets crack too, even with the most conscientious care and swabbing, so no point is proven. To keep the oboe bore clean and shiny, I recommend a cloth swab. Be very careful, however, of the size of the cloth. Make sure it is several inches longer than the joint, and experiment with the width until you get just the right width for the thickness of the cloth you are using. (See Photo 12.) It should pull through relatively easily. Due to the conical shape of the oboe bore, a larger swab must be used in the lower joint; so the oboe must be taken apart before drying (Photo 13).

The argument has been presented that to swab this small upper joint with a cloth will wear the bore and change its shape. This may be true, but to my knowledge it has not been proven. I think the "buildup" caused by lack of swabbing would be greater, faster and more detrimental than that caused by wearing of the bore with a cloth swab. It would be interesting indeed to know exactly how many million times one would have to pull a soft cloth through this very hard wood to wear the bore enough to make a measurable change. My guess would be that the instrument would be discarded due to key wear long before this would happen.

Most bassoonists use the long cotton-covered wire swabs, made in two different sizes especially for this instrument. They are easier to use than the "pull through" type. Even

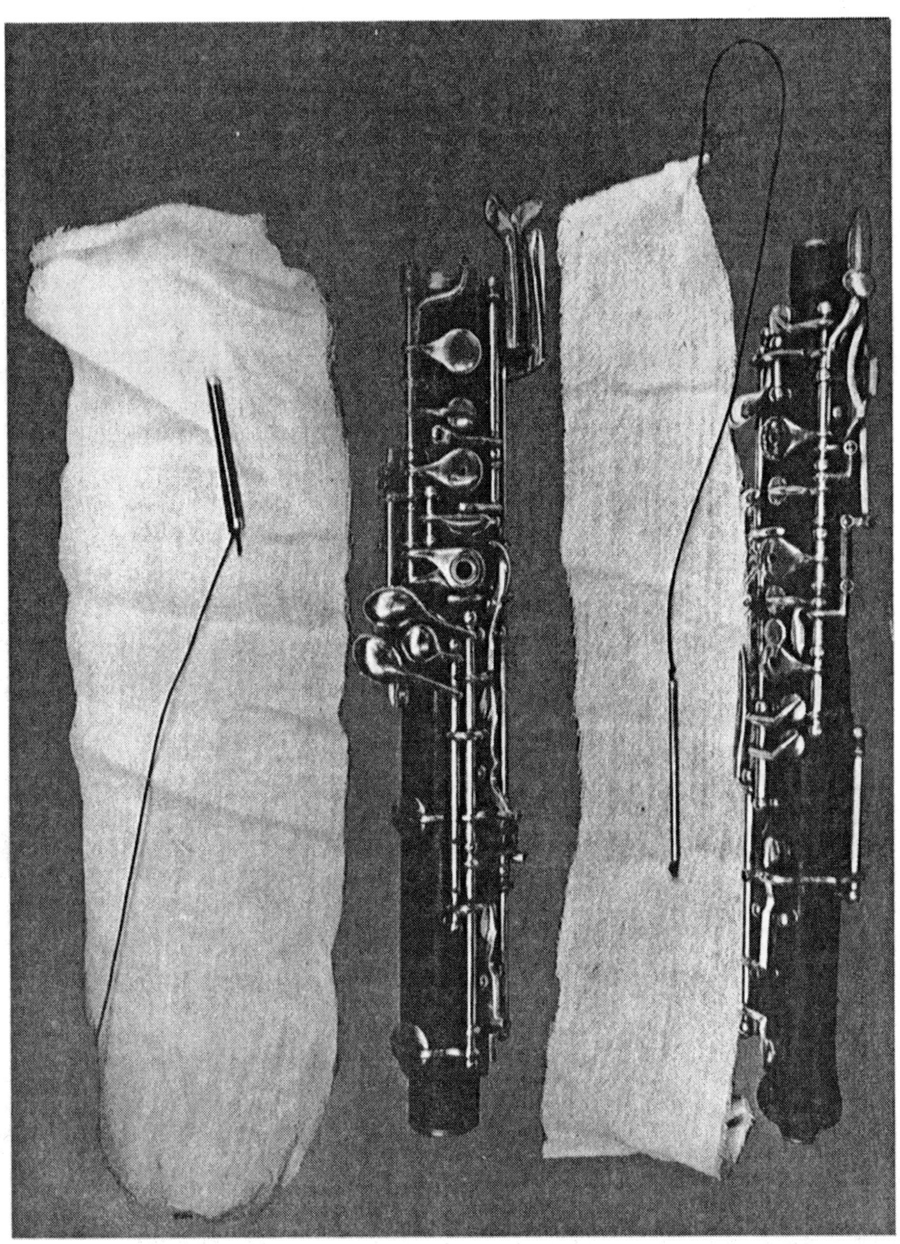

Photo 12. Homemade Oboe Swabs

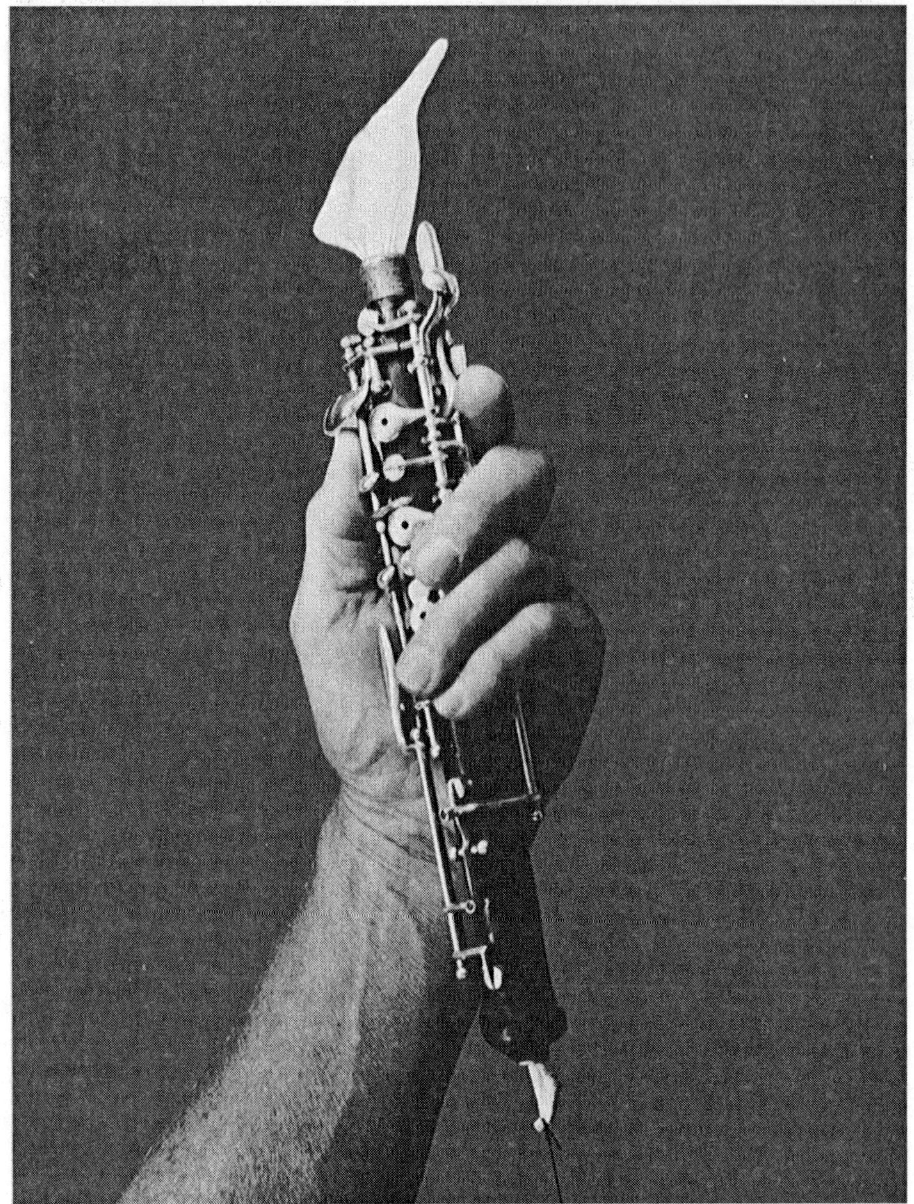

Photo 13. Swabbing the Oboe

though the tenor wing is usually lined, it should still be cleaned with the small swab every time the instrument is used. The bocal is extremely vulnerable to a critical "build-up" due to its small diameter. It is often neglected. The easiest way to keep it clean is to rinse it under a faucet as often as possible immediately after using. A small cylindrical brush, such as used on some electric razors, with the handle cut off and looped as shown in Photo 14 makes a good bocal brush. Tie about 10 inches of fish line to the loop in the brush and pull it through the bocal several times with soap and water. Remember that the whisper key tube extends about 1/8-inch into the bocal bore.

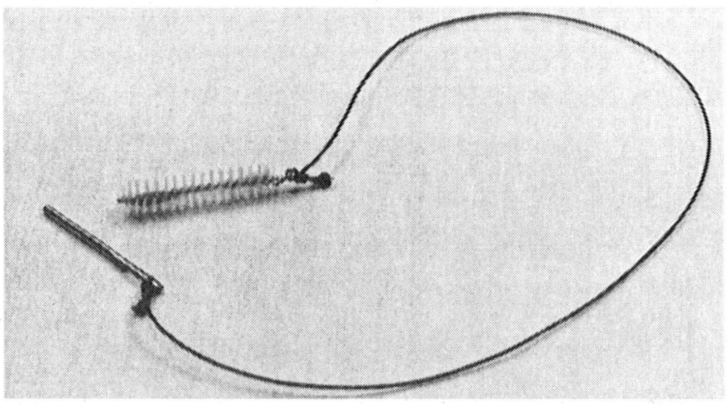

Photo 14. Brush for Cleaning Bassoon Bocal

Insist that your bassoon students empty the water that collects in the bow of the boot joint. In so doing, pour it down the side of the boot where it will not run into a tone hole. Failure to do this results in rapid deterioration of the pads and the eventual rotting of the wood at the bottom where the metal bow is attached. After emptying, swab both sides clean and dry with the larger of your two swabs. Usually no moisture reaches the bass wing. If you do clean this side, swab it first before your swab has picked up moisture from the boot.

Using the cleaning rod furnished with a flute, thread a piece of soft cloth, about 6 inches by 12 inches, through the eye, as seen in Photo 15; then over the tip, completely covering the rod with the cloth to avoid scratching the bore (Photo 16). The cloth should be long enough to cover the butt of the rod also, so that as you swab, you are holding on to both cloth and rod as shown in Photo 17. Leave the cloth on the rod and store it inside the body to minimize damaging the keys with a loose rod in the case. Wash the head joint once a week with a small bottle brush, soap and water.

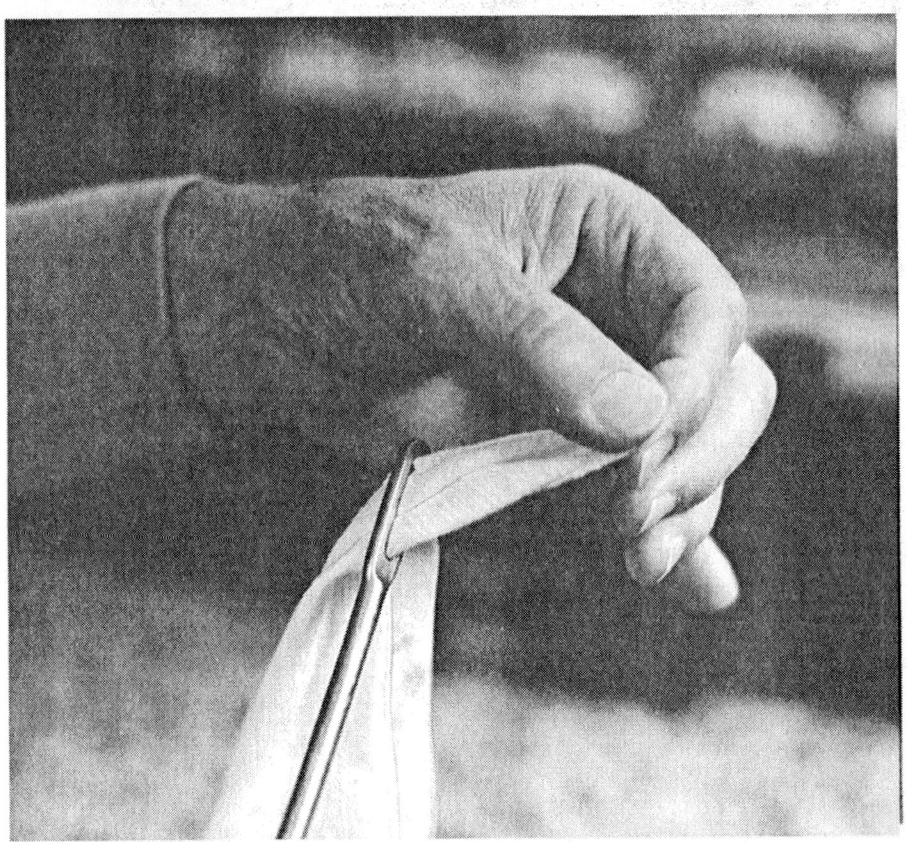

Photo 15. Thread Cloth Through Eye of Flute Cleaning Rod

Photo 16. Cloth Brought Over End of Rod

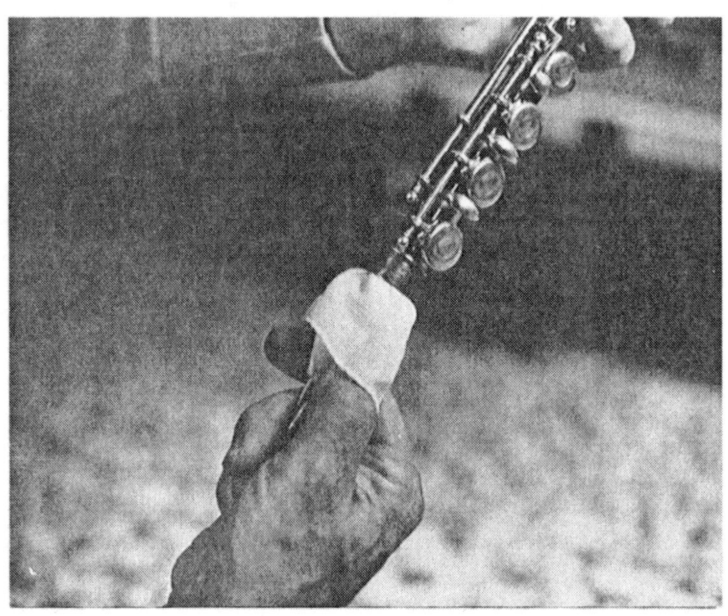

Photo 17. Rod and Cloth Held While Swabbing

Alto and tenor saxophones should also be swabbed after using. There are commercial swabs that are available, or a cloth and weight of appropriate size may be used as in Photos 18 and 19. Be sure to empty the water from the bell bow before laying the instrument on its side in the case. Once a week, remove the neck octave key and wash the inside of the neck with a sax neck brush, soap and water. There is no danger of damaging the lacquer unless you let the neck soak in a strong detergent. If you wash it immediately after playing there is no need to let it soak. Instruct your students always to remove the mouthpiece from the neck and wipe the mouthpiece dry with a cloth used only for the mouthpiece. Swab the body before storing in the case. Do not try to pull a cloth swab through a sax neck because the octave tube extends down 1/4-inch into the bore and would snag the cloth. About the best you can do with a baritone sax is to see that the water is emptied from the top crook every time, and the mouthpiece and neck kept clean.

In situations where proper maintenance has not been in effect, a buildup of lime corrosion, sugars and particles from dried saliva will have formed in mouthpieces, sax necks, alto and bass clarinet necks, bassoon bocals, etc. They should be cleaned as follows:

In a wide-mouth glass, stoneware or heavy plastic container that you can cover tightly, pour 1 quart of water. Slowly pour 1 quart of muriatic acid into the water. Be very careful not to let any acid splash into your eyes, and be sure to pour the acid into the water. If the container will not hold 2 quarts, keep the proportions 50-50 in any amount your container will hold and mix in the same manner. This mixture must be kept tightly covered when not in use or the fumes from it will rust nearby tools. Handle it with care and label the container.

Using canning tongs or a copper wire hook, immerse the object to be cleaned in the solution for a few seconds. Remove, rinse with cold water and then wash with warm water and soap or detergent. To avoid warping the lay, never use hot water on a woodwind mouthpiece.

Photo 18. Appropriate Size Sax Swab

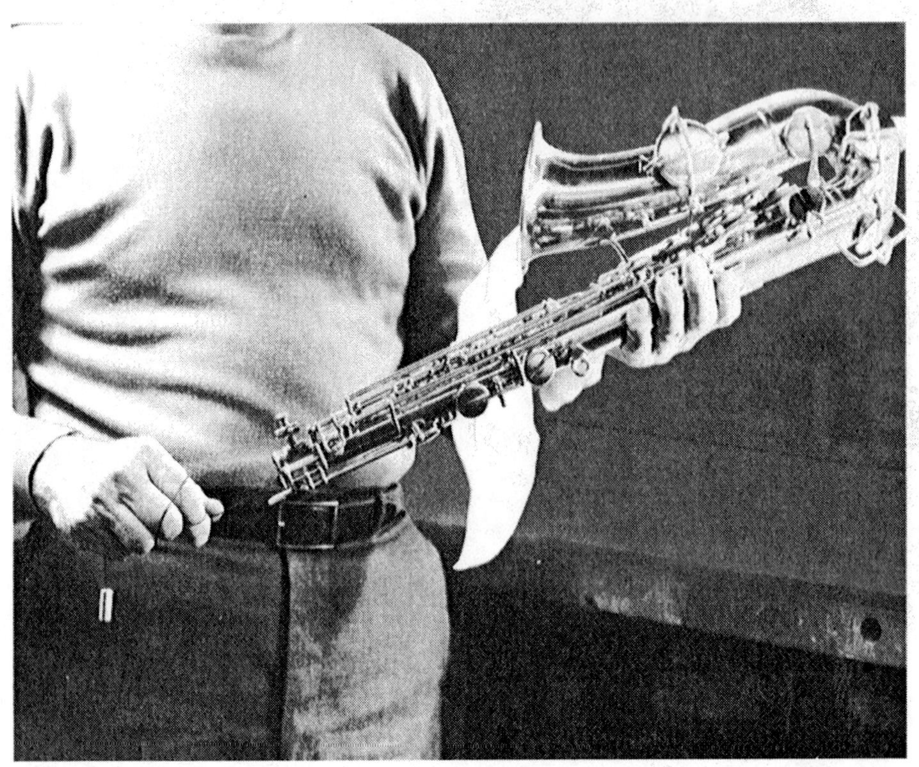

Photo 19. Swabbing the Saxophone

This solution will not harm the lacquer or the cork, and will usually clean the inside in a few seconds. Repeat the operation several times, if needed, rather than leaving it in the acid for more than a few seconds.

It seems logical that the manufacturers of wooden instruments know what care is best for their products. Most of them recommend the use of bore oil. Some repairmen refuse to oil a bore, claiming that the wood has absorbed all the oil possible before factory release. This point of view may be true. I personally do not know, but prefer to shine the bore of a wood instrument with a few drops of bore oil when I overhaul it. Most young students use too much oil in trying to follow manufacturers' instructions, thus causing early discoloration and deterioration of the pads. Recommend to your students that they use so little bore oil at each application that there is no chance of it running into a tone hole where it can reach a pad. It is useless to cover the pads during this oiling process as some repair books suggest, for the simple reason that should oil reach the pad seat it would wet the pad when the plastic or wax paper is removed. It is next to impossible to clean oil from a pad seat without removing the key because you must clean the tone hole as well as the seat.

Oiling the key mechanism is an absolute must if you are to avoid future costly repairs. Purchase a hypodermic needle type oil bottle and invite your students to use it. (Photo 20.) This job should normally be done twice a year, but if your band plays night football games, the key mechanism should be oiled every three or four weeks during the football season because of the condensation of moisture when the cool evening air contacts a breath-warmed instrument. In lieu of such an oiler, keep a shallow container of oil and a fairly large needle spring on your bench for this purpose. Use a shallow container, as shown in Photo 21, so that the needle cannot be immersed more than 1/4-inch to insure that the drop of oil picked up will be a small one. Touch every

Photo 20. Oiling Each Pivot

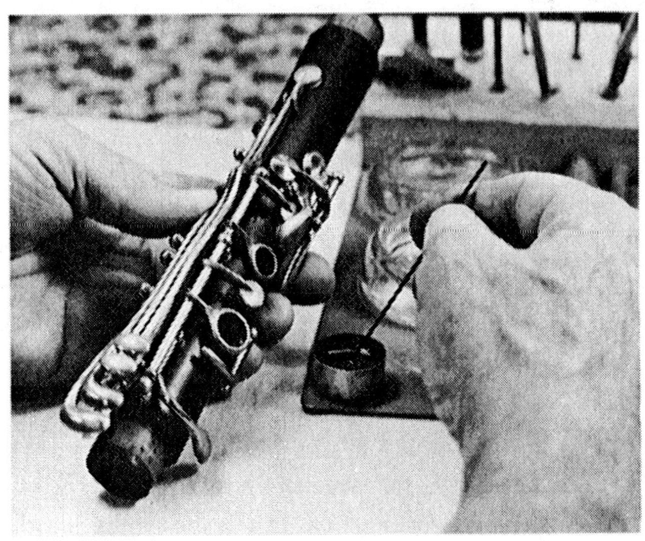

Photo 21. Shallow Container for Oil

movable contact on the mechanism with a tiny drop of oil on the needle point. You can prevent the springs from rusting too, by keeping them lightly oiled. Too much key oil makes the instrument dirty and messy to handle, but no oil at all really spells trouble. I have never felt it necessary to use regular key oil. Any light electric motor oil or "3-in-1" will do the job.

Repair Notes

3

WOODWIND MOUTHPIECE MAINTENANCE

It is hard to believe that anyone would put a mouthpiece into his mouth in the condition in which I find many that come into my shop. There are two prime reasons why you, as a teacher, should take a few minutes in instructing your students as to proper care and handling of this most important part of their instrument. First, any appreciable buildup here will affect tone quality and pitch. Second, from a sanitary standpoint, it is difficult to find a more effective culture for the growth of bacteria. I have used the following procedure with my own mouthpieces and with my students for over 40 years:

Keep a separate piece of cloth in the case for the mouthpiece only, and insist that the student dry his mouthpiece with it following every session. This cloth should be about one-half the size of a man's handkerchief, and should be of old cotton so that it is relatively soft and thin. Use no weights.

Twist a corner of the cloth and push it in the mouthpiece window from the tip end. When it shows at the other end pull it slowly through and back several times until the mouthpiece is dry and clean. (See Photo 22.) AVOID contact with the tip rail as much as possible. Laundering this cloth every week will help keep it sanitary.

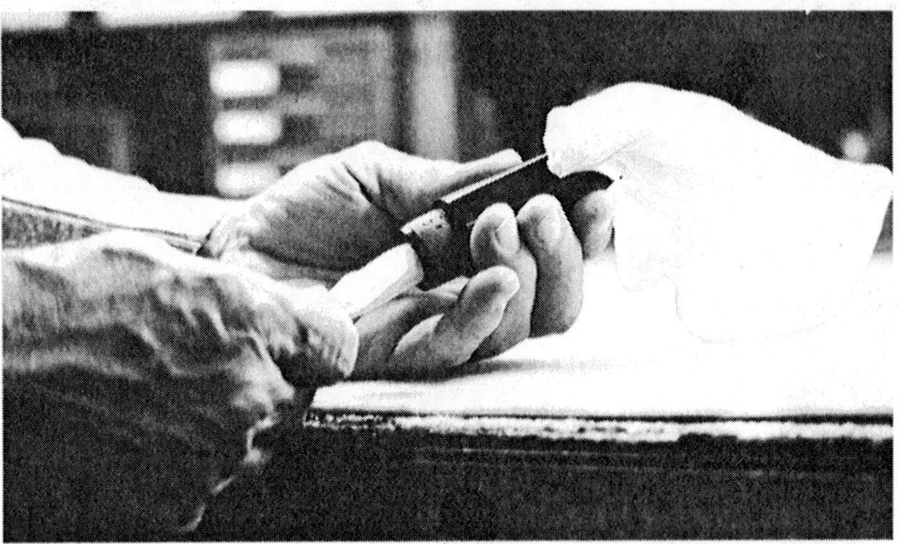

Photo 22. Cleaning a Woodwind Mouthpiece

To remove the hardened deposit built up inside a mouthpiece due to failure to keep it clean, immerse the mouthpiece into a 50-50 solution of muriatic acid and water as described on page 22. Remove, rinse with cold water and wash with a mouthpiece brush and soap. In using a mouthpiece brush be very careful not to scratch the baffle or the tip rail. A discarded plastic toothbrush narrowed to one or two rows of bristles makes an excellent substitute for a mouthpiece brush and presents little danger of scratching the mouthpiece. Hot water can be extremely hazardous, as it will soften rubber or plastic to the extent that the lay can be easily warped and damaged.

Do not attempt to acid-clean a mouthpiece that has a plastic inlay for a tooth rest as the acid affects the adhesive that holds the inlay.

A pair of wire tongs is necessary to immerse and remove the mouthpiece, or in lieu of tongs bend a piece of wire into an "S" and hook the objects.

Teach your students to be very careful in positioning the ligature and cap. A good policy is to leave the ligature on the mouthpiece and just slide it up far enough to slip the butt of the reed down under it. Teach them to cap the mouthpiece in slow motion.

A mouthpiece with damaged tip or side rails can often be made playable. Using a piece of plate glass as a base, lay a quarter sheet of 500 or 600 grit wet or dry abrasive paper on the glass. Remove the burr by pulling the mouthpiece as shown in Photo 24, no more than 1/4 to 1/2-inch toward the tip and in a rocking motion upward following the curvature of the lay. If the burr is on the tip rail only, try to keep the side rails from any contact with the paper.

A magnifying glass or jeweler's loupe is handy to determine whether the burr has been removed. In spite of the fineness of the paper, it will cut a mouthpiece very rapidly, and you can easily change the facing by removing more than the burr itself.

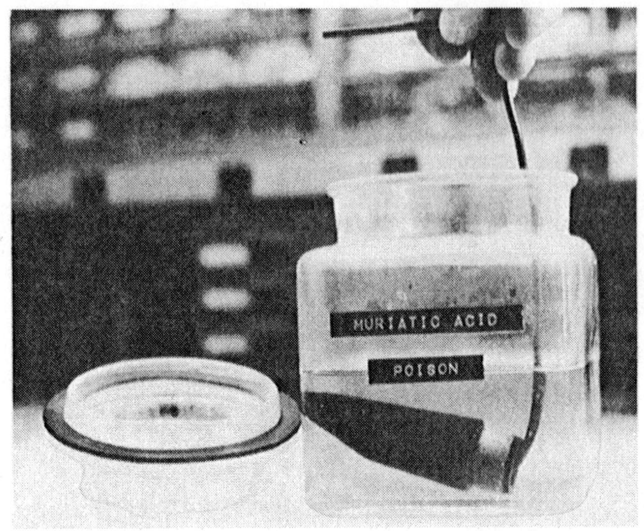

Photo 23. Removing Hardened Deposit from Mouthpiece

Photo 24. Removing Tip Rail Burr

4

TIGHTENING LOOSE SOCKET RINGS

During the cold months the dry heat in our homes and schools removes some of the moisture from wood instruments causing them to shrink. Consequently, about January or February, in climate where much heating is necessary, you will find instruments with loose socket rings. Caution your students to NEVER assemble an instrument with a ring loose enough to be moved with your fingers. The rings are there to keep the thin wood of the socket from splitting when the tenon is inserted, and play of even one or two thousandths of an inch between the ring and the wood is inviting a split socket. Proceed as follows:

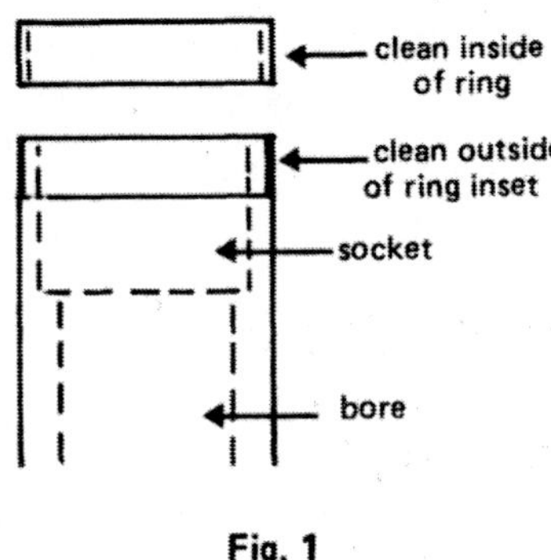

Fig. 1

Remove the loose ring and clean the inside of the ring and the ring inset on the socket. Leave no residue of cloth, paper or adhesive. A few manufacturers raised burrs on the inside of the rings to hold them on when the wood shrinks. This defeats the whole purpose of the ring. File such burrs until the inside of the ring is smooth. Most rings are tapered slightly. Be sure to replace them with the small end of the taper up toward the open end of the socket. Cover the end of the socket with a small piece of cloth, as shown in Photo 25.

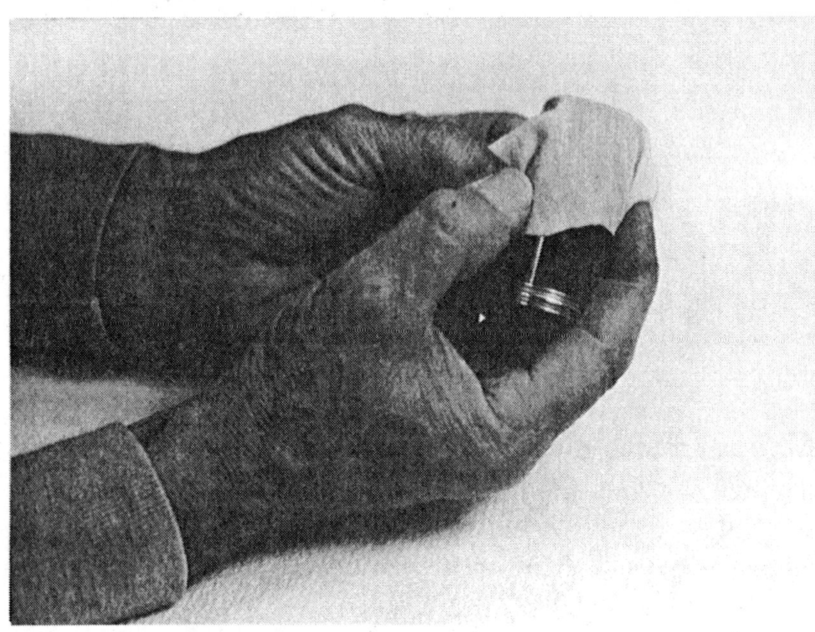

Photo 25. Socket End Covered With Cloth

Place the clean ring, small end of the taper up, over the cloth. You should be able to just start the ring on with your fingers. If you cannot do this, the cloth is too thick. If you can push it on with your hands for more than 1/16-inch, the cloth is too thin. The thickness of this piece of cloth is very important as it is possible to shrink the socket with too thick a cloth to the point where the tenon cannot be inserted. Try using a piece of old cotton, such as a handkerchief or bedsheet that has been washed many times.

Once the ring is started on with your fingers, use a rawhide mallet and drive it down evenly all the way around until about 1/32-inch from the inset shoulder. Drive it slowly with light blows and hold the part in your hand rather than resting it on a solid surface. With a razor blade or sharp knife, cut off the cloth between the ring and the inset shoulder, as seen in Photo 26. Cut it tightly to the ring and leave no ravelings.

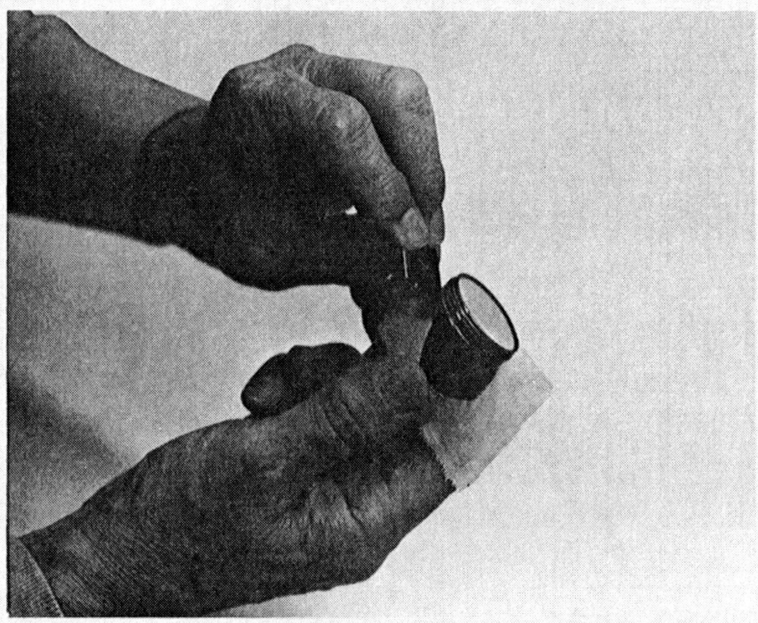

Photo 26. Cutting the Cloth Tight to the Ring

Pierce the taut cloth over the end. With your knife under the cloth and over the end of the socket, cut the circle of cloth from the top (Photo 27). Be careful not to cut or scratch the end of the socket shoulder. Finish by driving the ring completely down to the inset shoulder. If you have trimmed the cloth cleanly there will be no visible indication that the ring has been replaced.

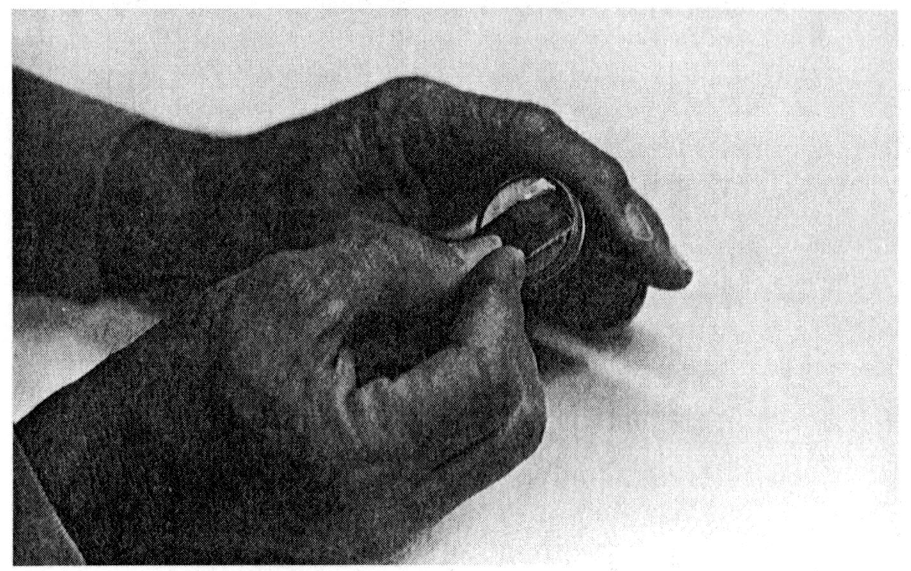

Photo 27. Trimming the Cloth from Top

Great caution should be used to avoid tightening the ring to the point where the matching tenon will not fit. If this should happen you may sand either the tenon or the inside of the socket or both until they will go together. Usually if you have over-tightened the ring to this extent you will chip the inset shoulder and mar the ring if you try to remove it. Consequently, it is better to use a cloth a bit too thin than one that is too thick. After you have tightened several, you will learn the approximate thickness of cloth to use depending upon the degree of looseness of the ring.

In my estimation this method of tightening rings is superior to shrinking the ring in a press because that few thousandths of an inch thickness of cloth gives a resilient but firm contact with both wood and metal allowing for some change in the size of wood while still letting the ring serve its intended purpose of protecting the thin wood of the socket.

Inasmuch as most of the cracks in wood clarinets occur at the top of the upper joint below the tenon, it would seem reasonable to me for the manufacturers to place an additional ring at this point. It would look strange at first to see two rings together, one on the bottom of the barrel and one on the top of the upper joint, but I think it would prevent some cracks. If this were done during the manufacturing process and before the final reaming it would remove the danger of bore distortion often caused by banding after the instrument has cracked.

Unless the ring on the bottom of the bell is so loose that it rattles, do not be concerned with it. It does not protect the bell as the other rings protect a socket. This ring must be shrunk in a press in order to be properly tightened. You can stop the rattle with a few drops of Duco cement placed at intervals in the crack between the ring and the wood.

Repair Notes

5
TENON CORKING

Tenon corks on clarinet joints and saxophone necks should be correct size for secure placement. If the cork is properly lubricated and the fit is too tight, remove the lubrication with a paper towel and sand the cork by stropping with a strip of 220 grit emery cloth. Lubricate and try again for size. Repeat the sanding as needed.

If the cork is too small, but still intact and resilient, a repair may be effected by smoothly wrapping the cork with one or more layers of Scotch Magic Tape after removing as much of the lubrication as possible. Should the cork be broken or loose, remove it, scrape the tenon clean and replace with new cork.

Cork may be purchased from any of several instrument repair supply houses. It comes in 4 x 12 inch sheets and in seven different thicknesses. Saxophone necks and clarinet mouthpieces take cork 1/16-inch thick. Since these cork sheets are cut the long way with the grain, draw a line down the center of the length of each sheet to enable you to tell the way the grain runs. Then cut the sheet into three 4-inch squares. It is sometimes difficult to see a clearly defined grain flow in a sheet of cork.

To cork a tenon, cut a piece of cork the width of the tenon inlay and 4 inches long. You must judge whether to use 1/32nd or 1/16th thickness. When in doubt use 1/16th, as you can always work it down to the correct size. Always cut the strip with the grain. Bevel one end as shown in Photo 28. Coat the bevel, the bottom of the strip and the tenon inlay with contact cement (Photo 29).

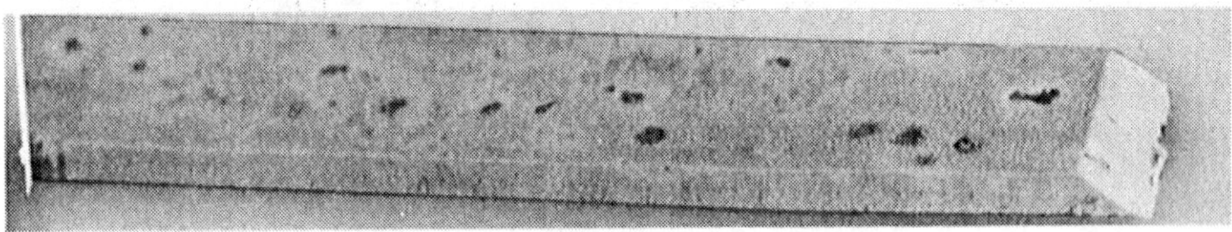

Photo 28. Beveled Cork Strip

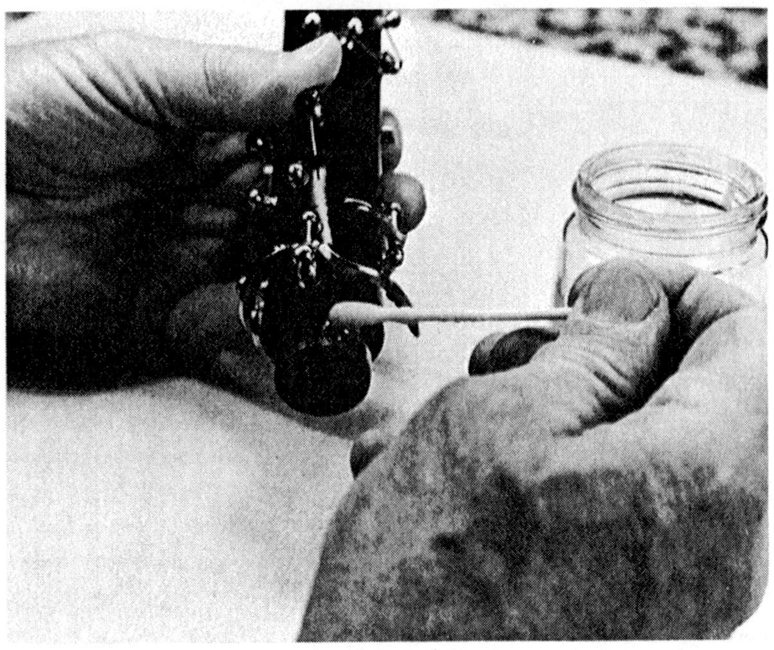

Photo 29. Coating Tenon Inlay with Contact Cement

Let the cement dry thoroughly. This usually takes 15 or 20 minutes depending upon the brand of contact cement used, the temperature of the room, and the humidity. When dry, apply to the tenon as shown in Photo 30, taking care to keep the strip at right angles to the joint and inside the inlay edges when first contact is made. Be sure to lay the beveled end down first (Photo 31), then come over the bevel with the other end of the strip (Photo 32).

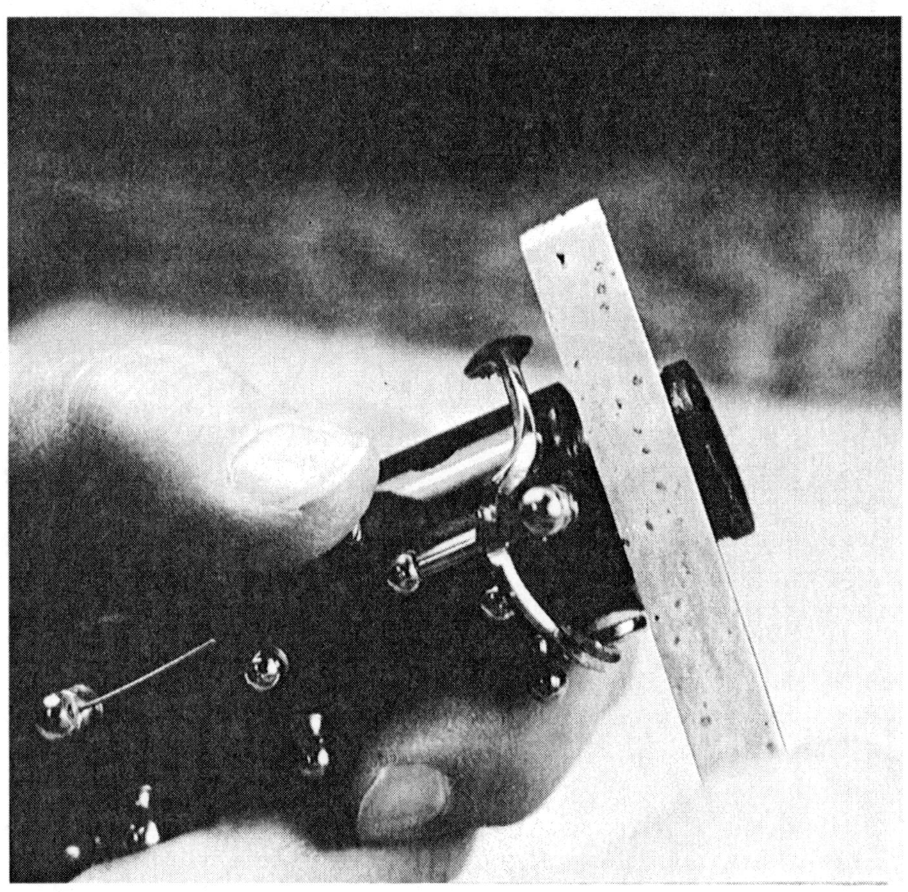

Photo 30. Applying Cemented Cork to Cemented Tenon

Photo 31. Beveled End Laid Down First

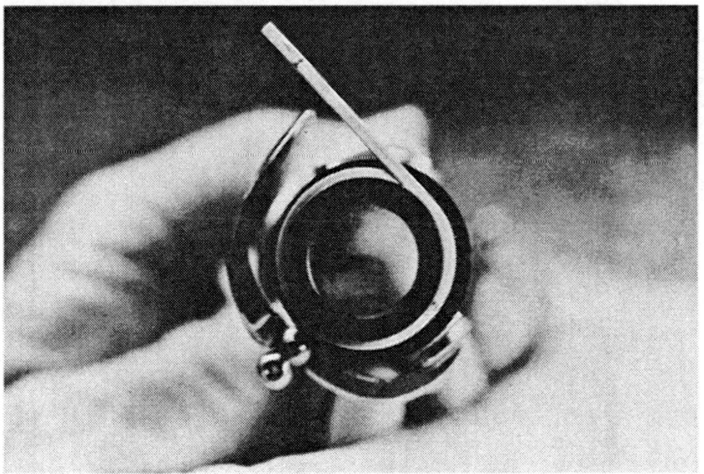

Photo 32. Bringing Strip Clear Around and Over Bevel

The cement on the top of the bevel will stick to the cement on the botton of the strip. Cut off the excess cork and bevel the leading edge of the strip as shown in Photo 33 to minimize the danger of tearing the leading edge loose in assembly.

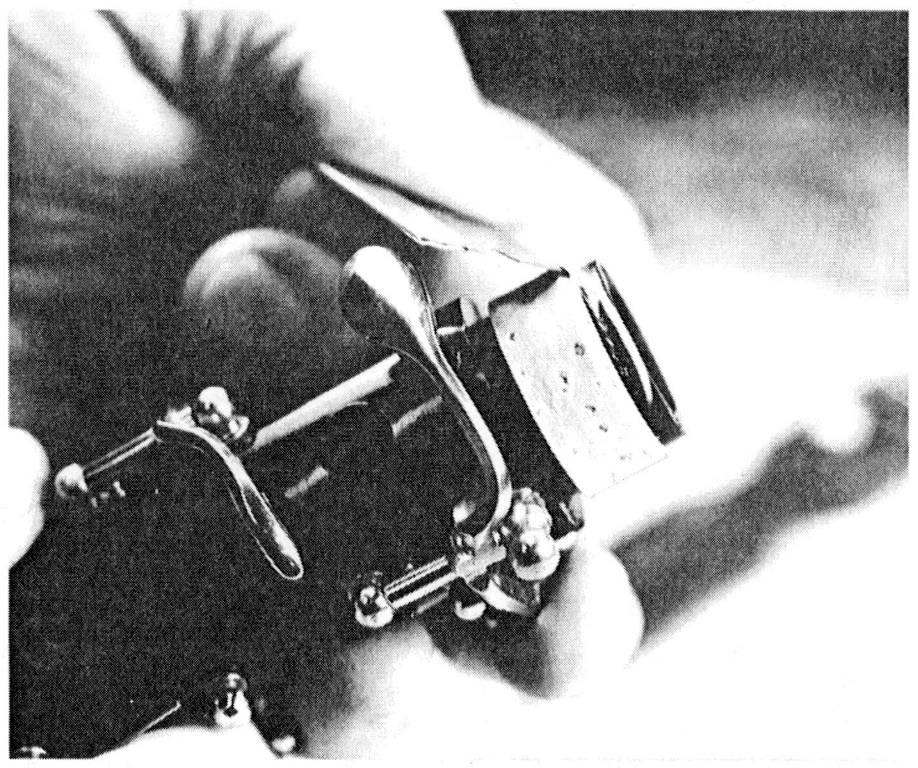

Photo 33. Beveling Leading Edge

Leave the trailing inside edge unbeveled to give more bearing surface thus lessening the chance of the joint rocking. Strop with a 1/2-inch wide strip of 220 grit emery cloth or file the cork down to correct size. In stropping, pull the emery AROUND the tenon to avoid sanding flat spots. In working the cork down to size, avoid all contact with the tenon itself.

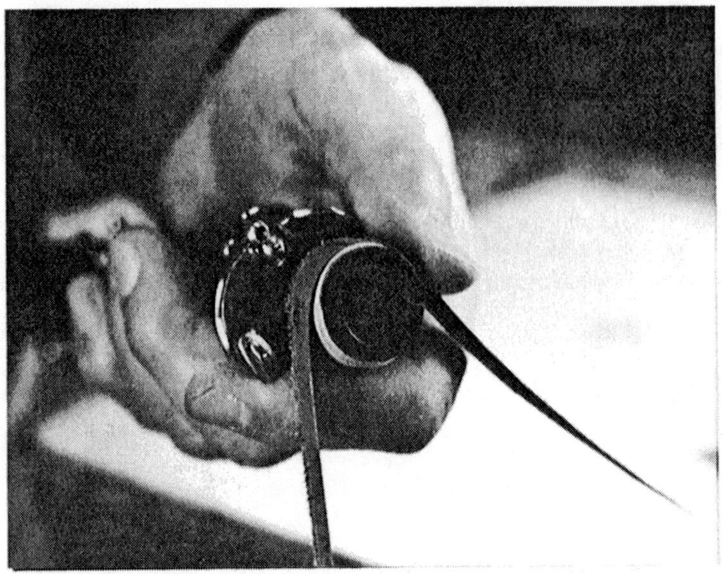

Photo 34. Proper Method for Stropping

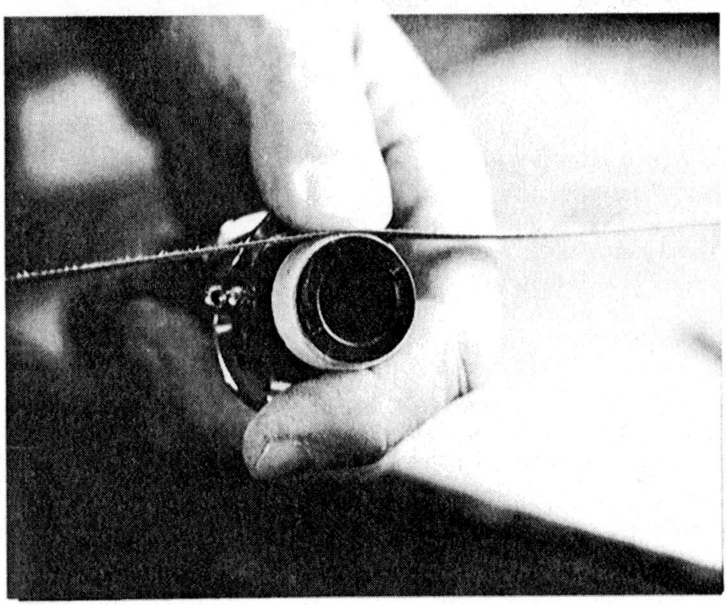

Photo 35. Improper Method for Stropping

Try the tenon with the cork ungreased in its proper socket. When the cork will start in and go about 1/8-inch with a little pressure, remove, grease the cork thoroughly and assemble. If you feel that the joint is too tight, remove the grease before further sanding. The fit should be tight, but should not require undue pressure to assemble. Never assemble with the tenon cork ungreased, or with the socket ring loose.

The cork on a saxophone neck is applied in the same manner. Cut a strip of cork about 1 1/2-inches wide with the grain and bevel one end. Apply to saxophone neck as shown in Photo 36. Because the sax neck is tapered, the cork will not meet in a perfect circle as you press it around the neck. Do not be concerned about the reinforcing ring soldered to the end of most sax necks. Let the cork come over the ring in applying (Photo 37). After cutting off the surplus overlap, trim it with a knife just inside the ring as shown in Photo 38 and even up the back edge (Photo 39). As with the clarinet tenon, bevel the leading edge and strop to size. Use a strip of emery paper about 1-inch wide.

Use the same procedure to cork a bassoon bocal, but squeeze the cork first in a smooth-jawed vise or hammer it on a smooth surface to minimize the chance of the cork breaking due to the small diameter of the bocal.

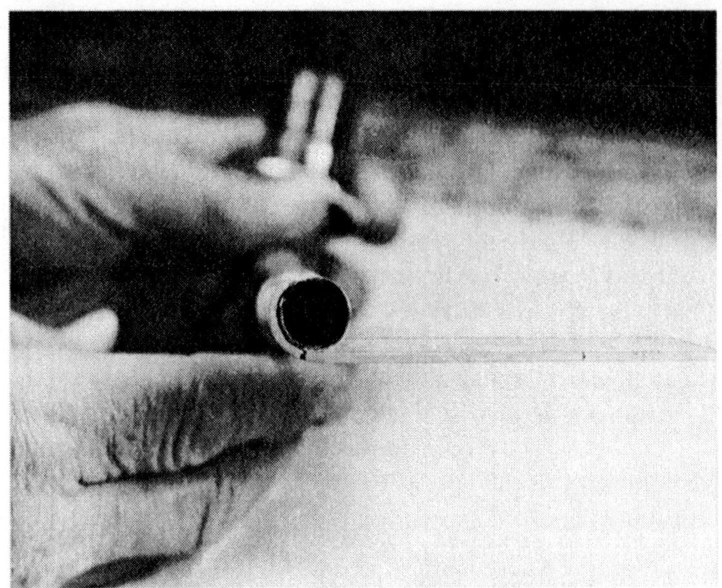

Photo 36. Corking Saxophone Neck

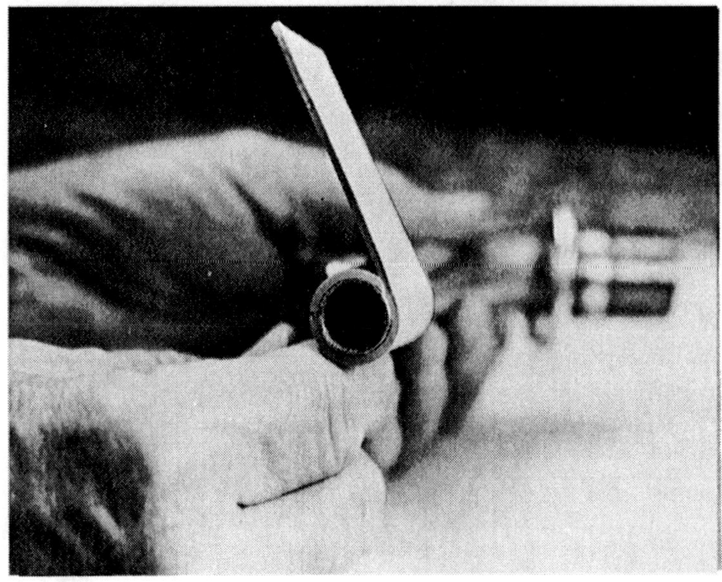

Photo 37. Letting Cork Come Out Over End Ring

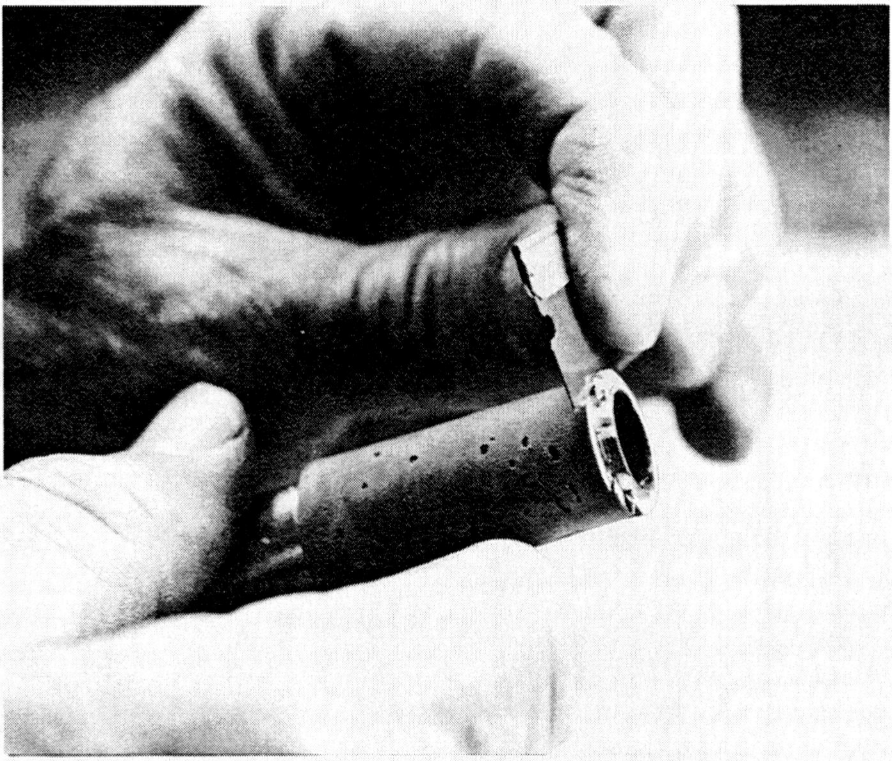

Photo 38. Trimming Just Inside the End Ring

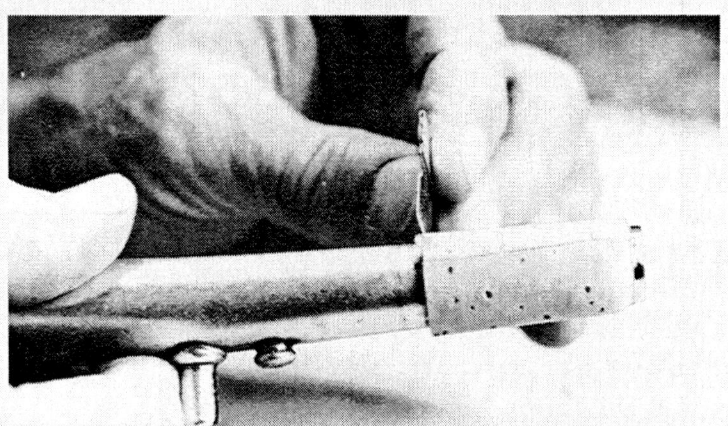

Photo 39. Evening Up the Back Edge

Repair Notes

6

REPLACING CLARINET PADS

Clarinet bladder pads are made with a disc of felt on a disc of cardboard. A thin skin of bladder is placed over the felt and is glued to the cardboard on the bottom holding the pad together. Good quality pads have two layers of this bladder skin, and in the very best pads the skin is treated to resist the deteriorating action of water and oil. All qualities are available in three different thicknesses, thin, medium, and thick in half millimeter steps ranging from 6 1/2mm to 20mm. This whole array again is multiplied by two in that you can get the pads beveled or not beveled. In a beveled pad, the cardboard disc is smaller than the felt disc and relatively thick, forming a shoulder. In a pad that is not beveled, the cardboard disc is thin, and the same diameter as the felt disc.

NOT BEVELED BEVELED

Photo 40. Clarinet Pads

Clarinet is the only instrument using a beveled pad, and even here the bevel is not necessary. Most repairmen, however, use the beveled pads on clarinet as they are easier to apply and adjust. In the list of supplies suggested in Chapter 1, medium thickness beveled pads are recommended.

Any pad with a break in the skin that reaches in to the seat will leak and should be replaced. The seat is that impression on the pad made by the shoulder of the tone hole. To replace this pad, you will need a new pad of the correct size, an alcohol lamp, pad slick, feeler gauge, pad cement, and a pin punch or needle.

In selecting a clarinet pad to replace the broken one, most novices make the mistake of fitting the cardboard disc to the pad cup rather than the felt disc. This means that the shoulder of the pad will rest on the edge of the cup making it very difficult to shift. Use as large a pad as possible but the felt disc should fit the cup (Photo 41).

PAD TOO LARGE PAD SIZE CORRECT

Photo 41. Correctly and Incorrectly Sized Pads

Although pads often can be replaced without removing the key from the clarinet, if time will allow it, remove the key so that you can chip the old cement from the cup. With your needle, make a tiny hole in the edge of the pad, as shown in Photo 42, to allow the warmed expanded air in the felt to escape so that the felt will take a seat. If the air cannot escape it is difficult to get a good impression of the tone hole on the pad. You can make the pad perfectly tight without this seat, but with the seat a greater area of the pad is in contact with the tone hole thus lessening to some extent the chance of a leak.

Some repairmen make the hole under the shoulder where the felt and the cardboard meet. The hole here is often sealed with cement.

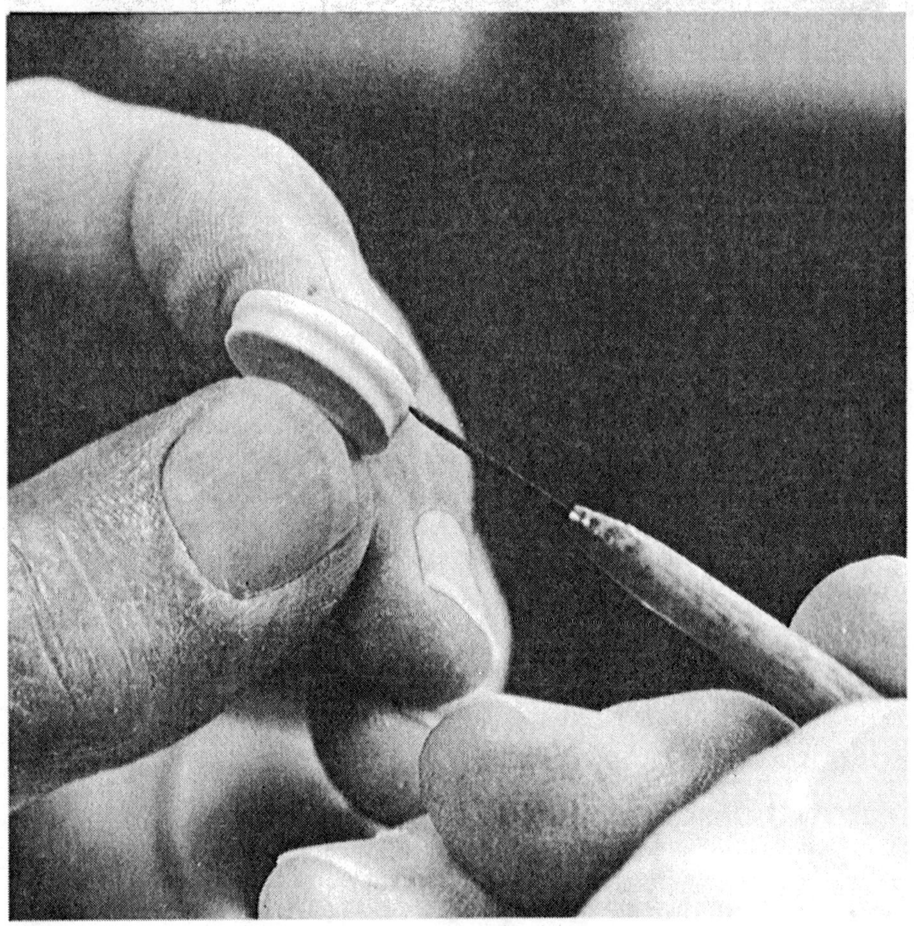

Photo 42. Pricking Edge of Pad

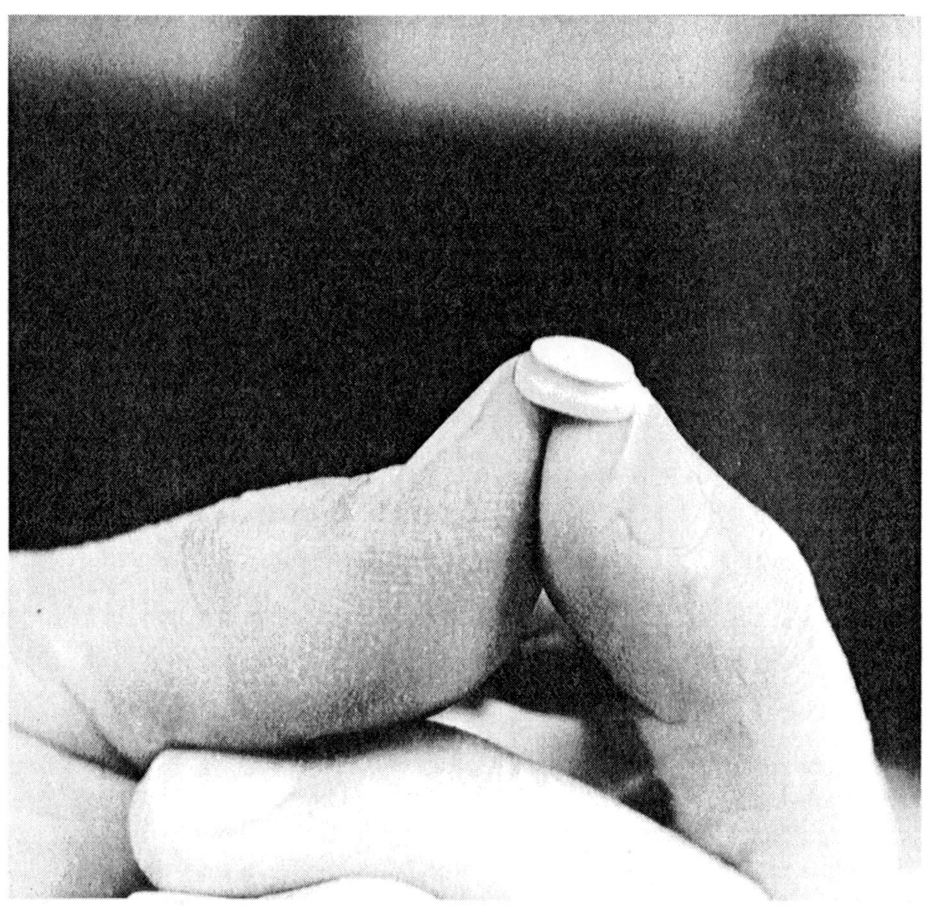

Photo 43. Holding Pad to Apply Cement

As shown in Photo 43, hold the pad on the tips of your thumb and second finger with your fingernails, apply melted cement to the cardboard disc. Cover the disc as evenly as possible and mound the cement slightly in the center. It is better to use too much cement than not enough as you can chip off the excess cement easily when the pad cup has cooled. Insufficient cement means there will be hollow spots in the cup, making the pad hard to level and multiplying the chances of its falling out in the future.

After you have dropped hot cement on your fingers a few times you will learn that by turning the cement stick over and back keeping it in motion will hold the melted cement on the stick until you can reach the pad with it. Hold your work close to the lamp to allow you to reach the pad as soon as possible.

Photo 44 shows the approximate amount of cement to use on the pad. This amount will vary according to the thickness of the pad and the depth of the pad cup. Use more cement to make the pad thicker, and less to make it thinner.

TOO LITTLE TOO MUCH ABOUT RIGHT

Photo 44. Examples of Cement Amounts on Pads

Heat the key cup and insert the cemented pad. The cup should be just hot enough to melt the cement and allow you to level the pad. A few seconds over the flame is usually enough for the small upper joint keys. The larger keys on the lower joint will take a slightly longer time to heat. The very small keys such as the A key and the top Eb-Bb key you may have to hold with pliers or tweezers to keep from burning your fingers. While the cement is still soft, use the pad slick to level the pad by eye in the cup. Replace the key on the instrument.

With the feeler gauge, test the pad in four places clear around the cup to determine where the pad is tight and where it is loose (Photo 45). In the case of an open key you must, of course, close it with your finger, and here is where many make their biggest mistake. Just bring the key down until it meets the tone hole. USE NO REAL PRESSURE.

By using pressure it is very possible to think the pad is hitting all the way around when in reality it may be quite light in one spot.

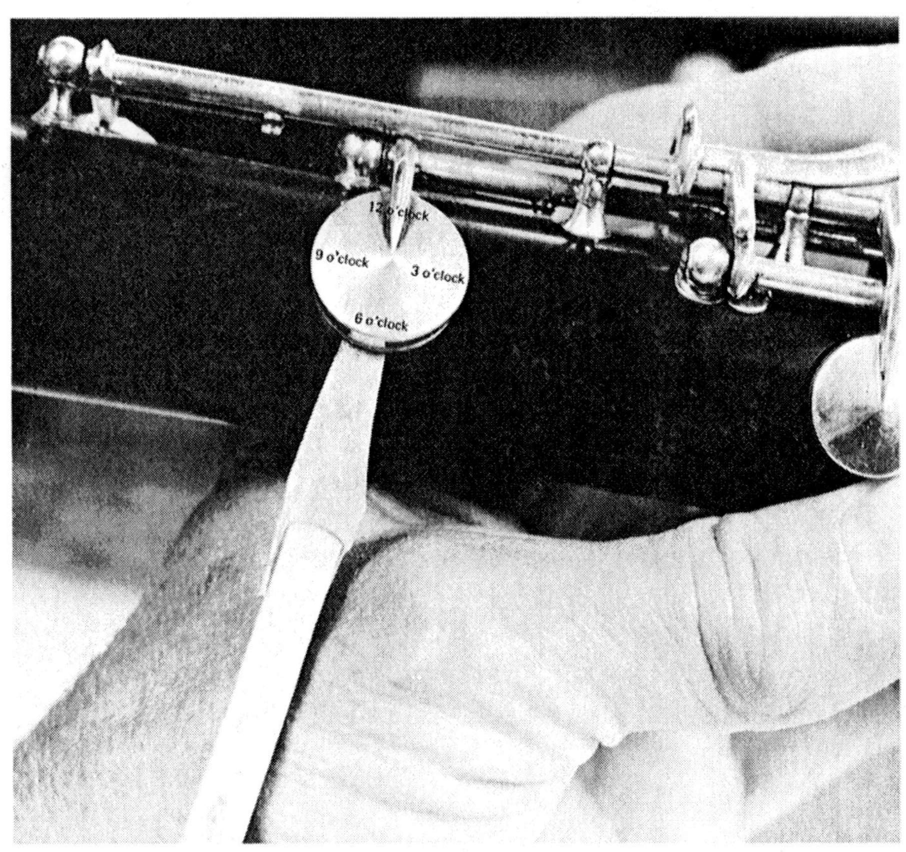

Photo 45. Testing with Feeler Gauge at 6 o'clock. (Also at 9 o'clock, 12 o'clock, and 3 o'clock.)

Photo 46. Cutaway of Pad with Too Much Cement

Photo 46 is a cutaway showing a pad with too much cement on it, making it too thick and causing it to hit hard in the back toward the hinge. Heat the cup as in Photo 47, and with the pad slick push the pad in at the back squeezing out cement and sliding the pad forward toward the front of the cup.

Should the pad be on one of the small top joint keys, either cut your feeler gauge to a taper of no more than 1/8-inch in width at the end, or use just a small corner, as it is easy to feel too much area at one time thus often missing the light drag area. After determining the area where the drag is light and where it is heavy (usually opposite sides) the pad must then be shifted in the cup until the drag is equal.

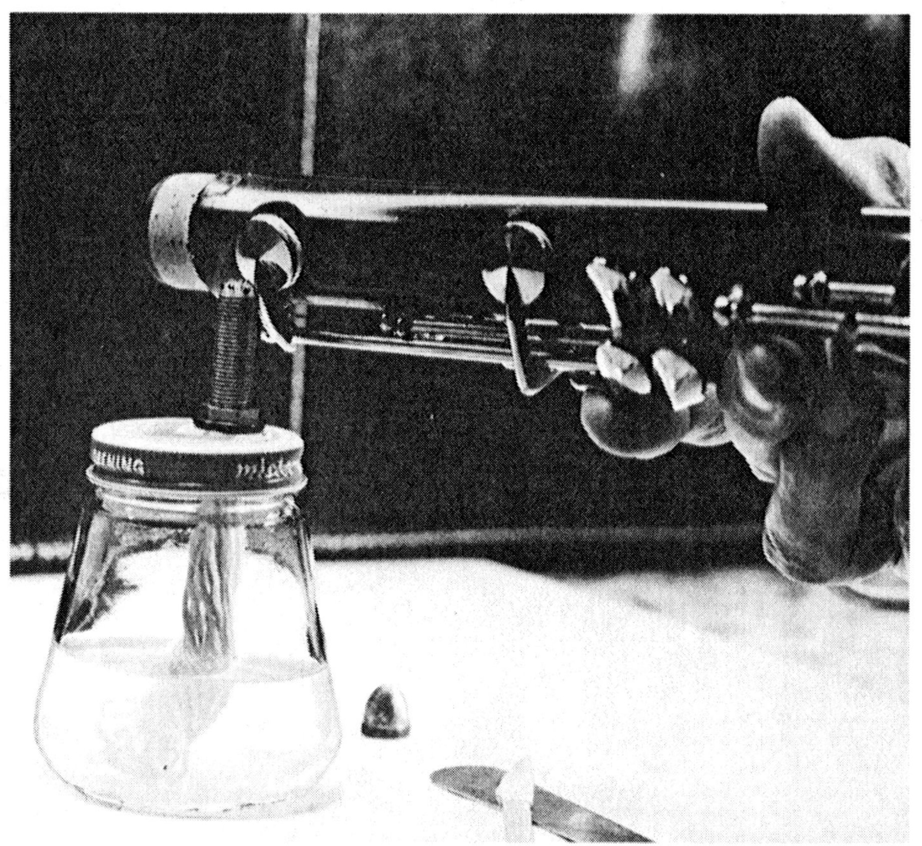

Photo 47. Using the Side of the Flame

Without removing the key from the instrument, heat the cup in the side of the flame while holding the key open. Using the side of the flame as in Photo 47 is extremely important. I know of no way to use the tip of the flame under the cup without danger of burning the clarinet, the pad, or both.

While the cup is still warm and the cement is soft, shift the pad with the pad slick by pushing up slightly into the cup that section of the pad that hits the tone hole the hardest. Due to the conical shape of the cup this pressure will shift the pad. Usually a beginner overshifts just as a beginning driver oversteers an automible for the first few times. Shift again as needed until the drag on the feeler is the same at all points.

Let the cup cool until the cement has hardened, then hold the key closed and apply pressure against the cup to seat the pad. If you apply this pressure too early before the cement is hard enough, the pad will shift to the back hitting hard near the hinge and lightly in front. Be sure to wait until the cup has cooled but the pad should still retain a little heat. This pressure will then force an indentation or groove in the pad to match the top rim of the tone hole. When the cup has cooled, chip off any cement that may have oozed out in the shifting process.

Except in an emergency when no new pad is available, do not attempt to replace an old pad that has fallen out as it is most difficult to get the seat aligned exactly as before. Use a new pad even though the old one may still be in good condition.

7
SPRINGS

When replacing broken needle springs, the removal of the broken stub can sometimes be a problem. If enough of the stub is left to allow a plier grip (1/4-inch or more), it can usually be removed by pushing on the pliers with your thumb as shown in Photo 48. It helps to tip the pliers from side to side a little while you push to loosen the tight wedged fit.

If there is less than 1/4-inch of the stub left, I recommend cutting it off about 1/32-inch from the post and then use round-nose pliers to force it back out (Photo 49). Be careful, of course, that the plier jaw on the post is either above or below the end of the spring to be removed.

When the spring is broken off flush with the post it must be removed with a punch and hammer. You can purchase spring punches, or you can make one by grinding the sharp point of a large needle spring flat, or by grinding a taper on any piece of tool steel such as a screwdriver blade or long hinge screw (Photo 50). These punches will need grinding nearly every time you use them because the springs are so hard they will quickly round over the face of the punch causing it to slip off the end of the broken spring. Before trying to remove a spring broken off flush, be very sure you know from which side of the post it originally extended as it must be forced out from that same side.

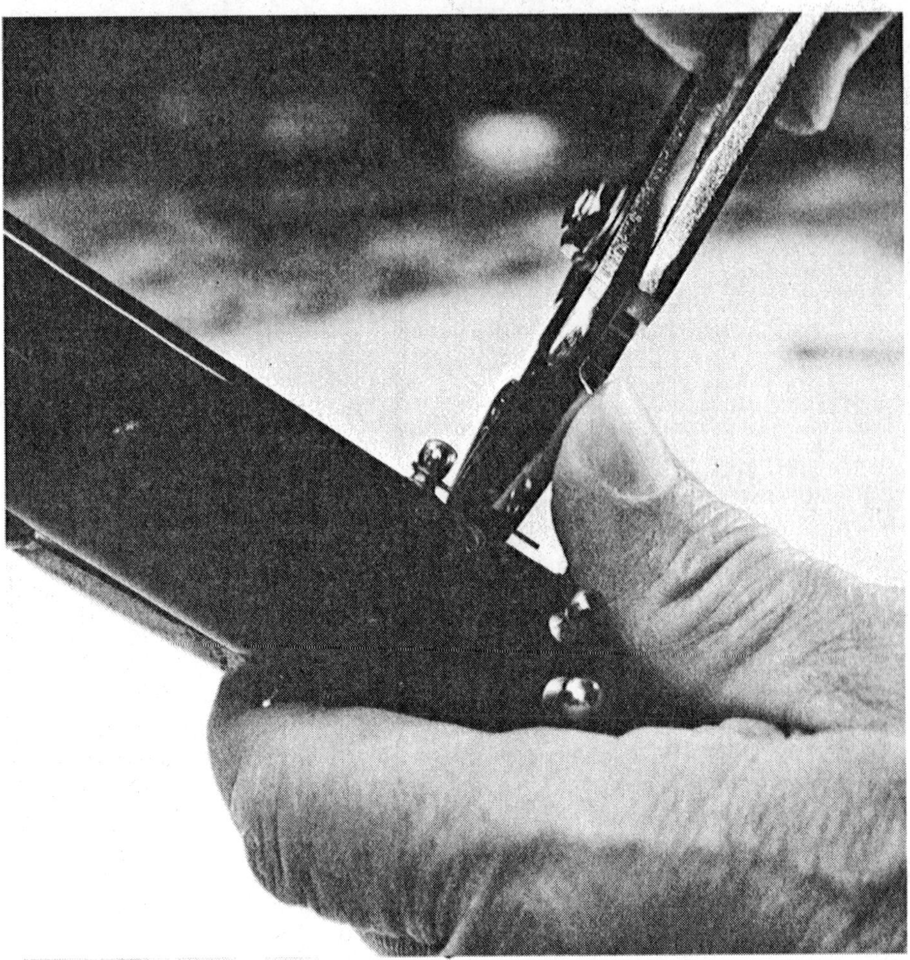

Photo 48. Pushing Out Broken Spring

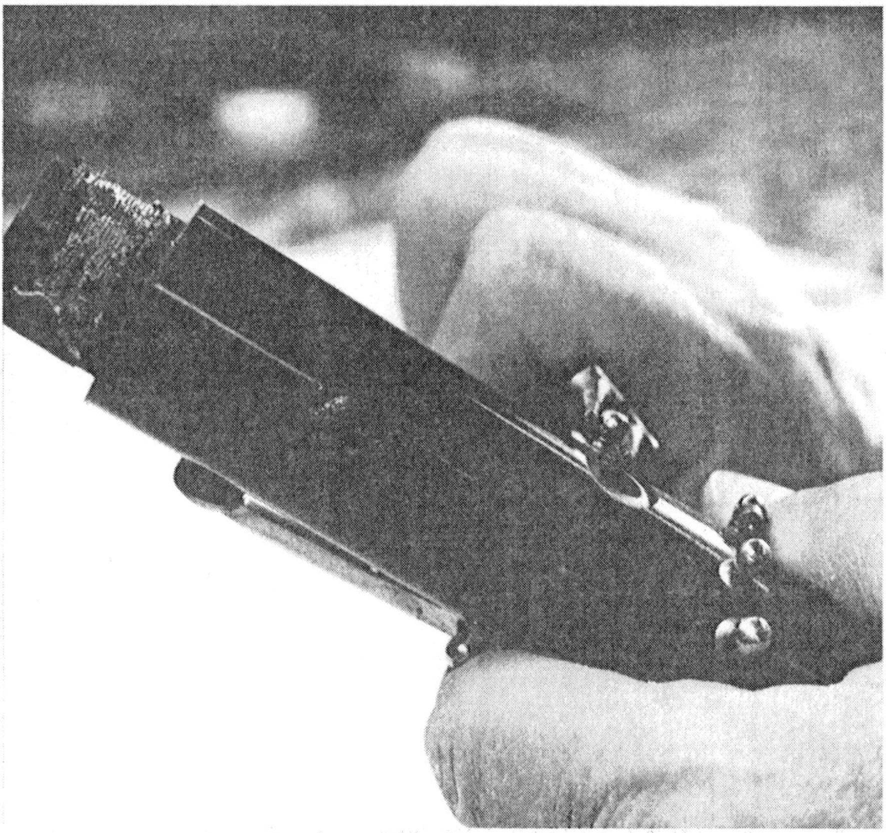

Photo 49. Removing Short Stub with Round-Nose Pliers

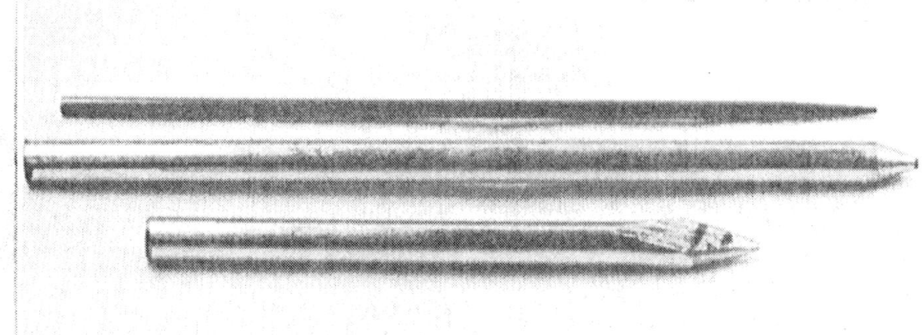

Photo 50. Homemade Spring Punches

Always support the back of the post on a lead or wood block when driving out a spring stub or you risk bending the post, knocking a soldered post completely off, or breaking out the post hole on a wood or plastic instrument (Photo 51). On an instrument where the post is threaded and screwed in, it is sometimes easier to remove the post from the instrument, then drive out the stub into the supporting block (Photo 52).

Photo 51. Punching Out Broken Spring Stub

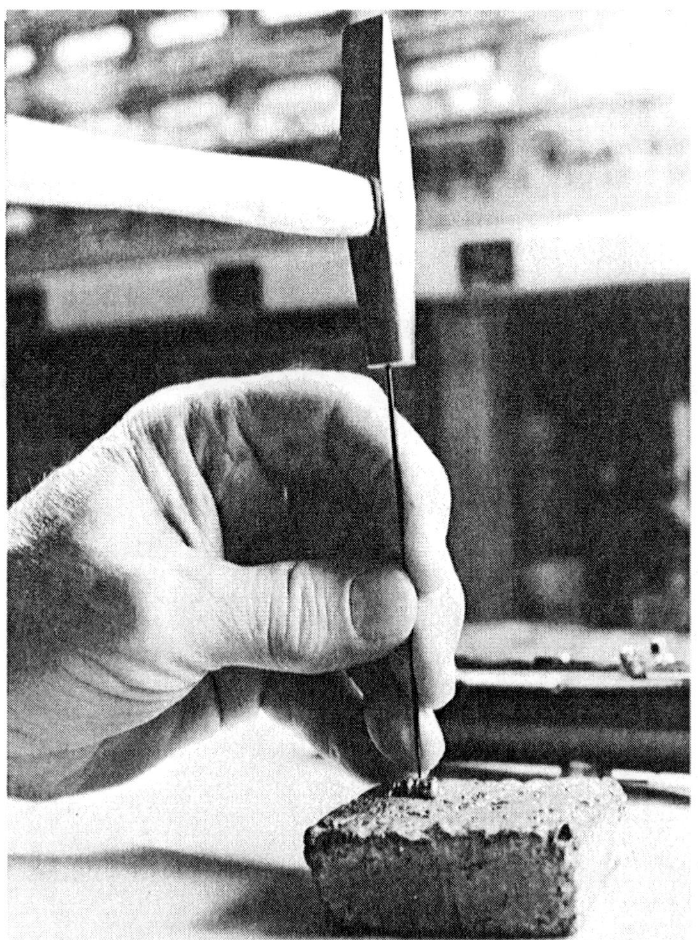

Photo 52. Driving Out Stub from Removed Post

When the post is soldered on, as with a flute or saxophone, an extra pair of hands to hold the instrument in position can be a big help. Be very sure your punch is on the broken stub when the hammer blow is delivered. It slips off easily unless both the broken spring and the punch points are flat. Sometimes it is necessary to file or grind the stub flat to keep the punch from slipping off and thus driving holes into the post.

After the stub has been removed, select the largest spring in your assortment that will go through the hole in the post. Determine how long it must be by measuring the post thickness plus the distance from the end of the key hinge to the spring hook. Add about 1/8-inch to this sum and cut the new spring to length using the tapered end of the spring. Be very careful when cutting a spring. You must hold on to both ends as shown in Photo 53 to eliminate the danger of eye damage from the flying spring.

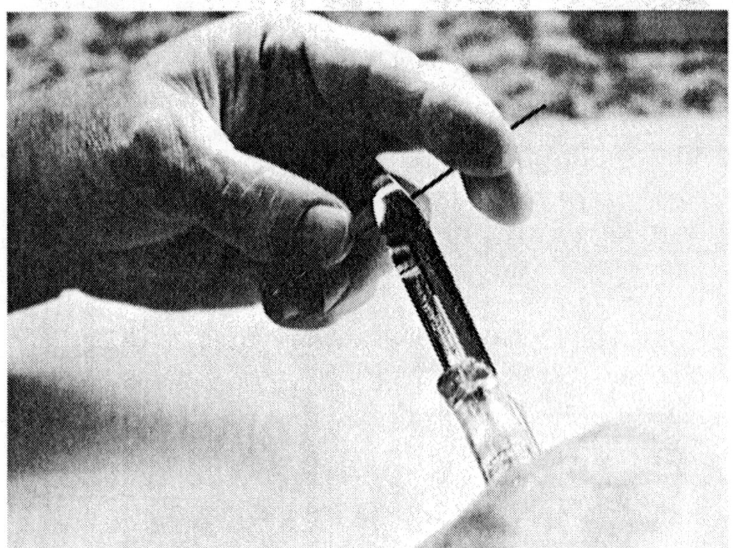

Photo 53. Cutting A Needle Spring

Using the edge of a hardened anvil, flatten the large end of the spring enough to bind it into the post with a press fit (Photo 54). This must be tight enough so that the spring cannot turn over in the post after it is curved to deliver the desired action. Press it into the post with pliers as shown in Photo 55. You will have trouble flattening the spring end on anything except a hardened anvil because the spring is so hard it tends to bury itself in cold rolled steel before it will flatten.

Photo 54. Flattening End of Spring on Anvil

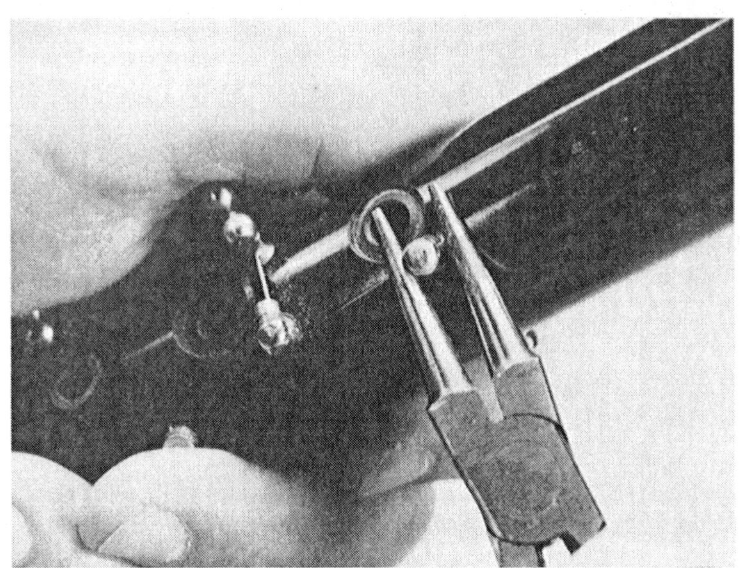

Photo 55. Pressing in New Spring

A gentle curve the full length of the spring will give better action and longer life than just one angle bent at the post. This type of curve can be made by tipping round-nose pliers in the direction you want the curve and then pushing the pliers the length of the spring with your thumb (Photo 56). Curve the spring toward the hole for an open hole key and away from the hole for a closed key.

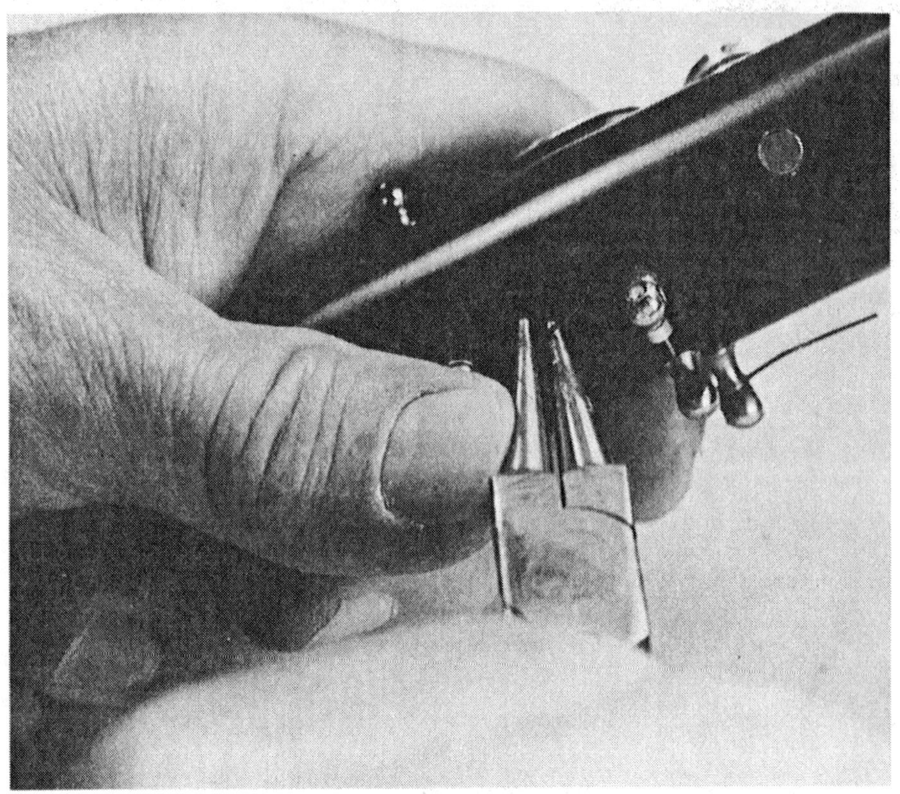

Photo 56. Curving the Spring

Because flute action is so much softer and lighter than clarinet or saxophone, do not use regular needle springs on a flute. Buy flute spring wire by the foot in four different sizes and install it as you would a needle spring.

Even though it might be necessary to use a rubber band as a spring substitute in an emergency, never leave one on a silver plated instrument. It will tarnish the plating in a few days and eat right through the plating in time.

Installing flat springs should pose no great problem. You may have to experiment some with the amount of bend in order to get the correct tension. Also, the location of the bend, whether it is ahead of or behind the hinge has everything to do with the correct action of the key. Be careful that the tip is not angled so that it digs into the wood. If more strength is needed than your assortment can supply, install another spring on top of the first. If it is too strong and you cannot get the correct tension by bending it, grind it narrower.

Repair Notes

8

REGULATING THE CLARINET

Cork is needed on the bottom of keys where they contact the instrument in order to regulate the height of the pad opening and to quiet the action.

With the use of contact cement, corking the keys has become a very simple procedure. Take pieces of 1/64-inch, 1/32-inch and 1/16-inch thick cork about 2 x 4 inches and give each a generous coating of contact cement on one side. Allow them to dry thoroughly. Be careful that the cemented sides do not touch each other for a day or two. For easy and efficient use of this cork, cut a strip about 1/4-inch wide from each piece and use up these strips rather than cutting into the edges of the larger pieces.

Unlike the procedure used in corking tenons, no cement is needed on the key to be corked. Heat that spot on the key that requires corking and apply the cemented cork. The heat will activate the contact cement binding it to the key (Photos

57 and 58). Trim excess cork from the key with a very sharp knife as shown in Photo 59. Slide the knife with a downward motion toward the key rather than trying to push it through the cork. Cemented cork is difficult to cut cleanly. Always slide the knife toward the key to avoid pushing the cork off from a key that is still warm. A slight taper away from the key edge makes a good looking job especially on cork thicker than 1/32-inch.

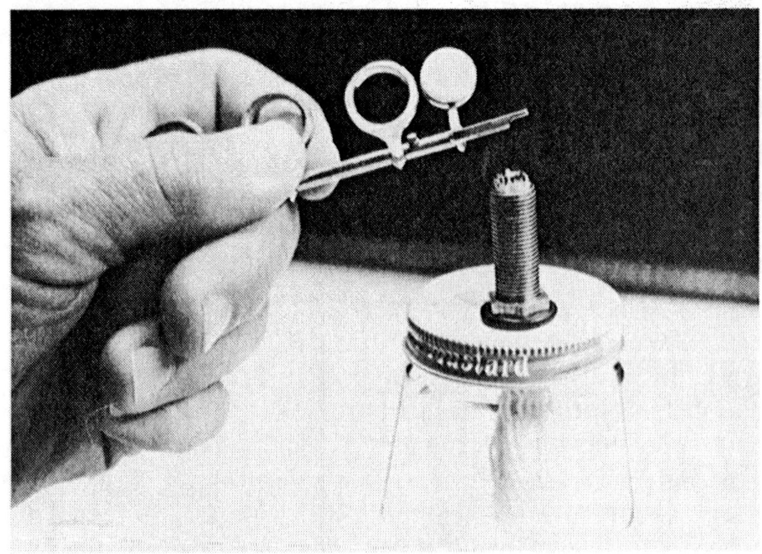

Photo 57. Heating Key for Corking

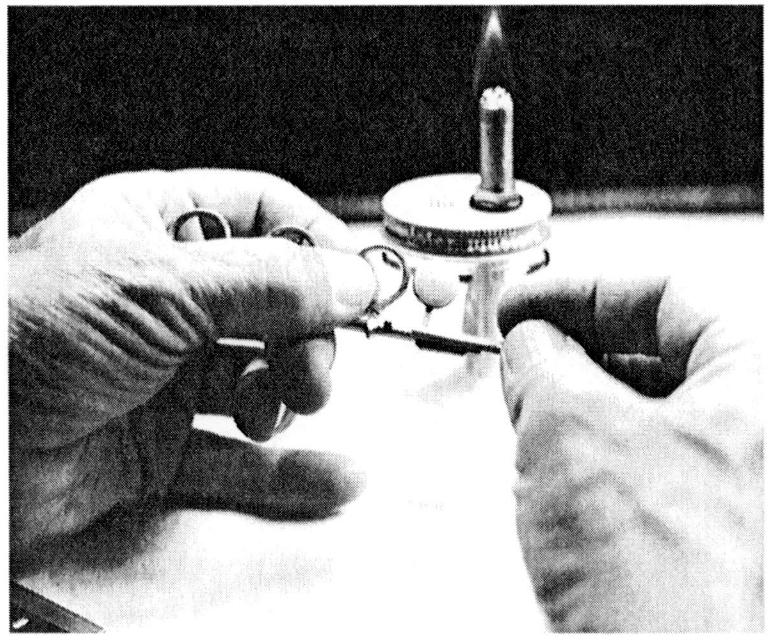

Photo 58. Applying Cork Strip to Heated Key

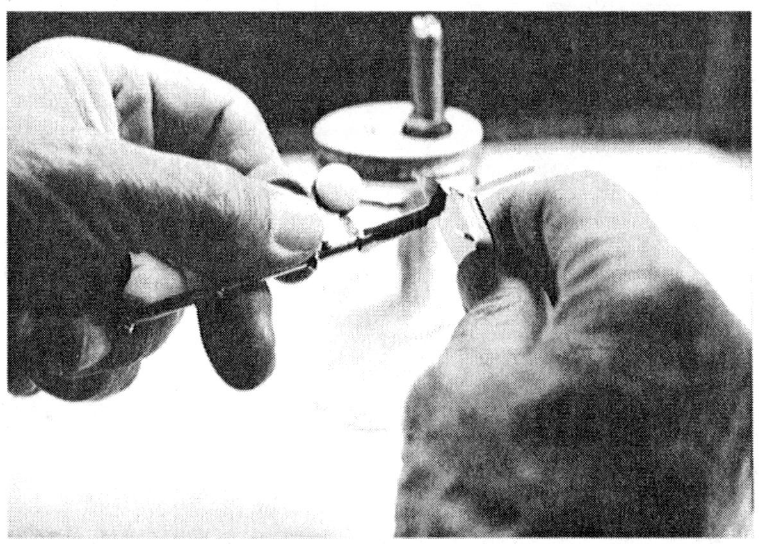

Photo 59. Trimming to Size

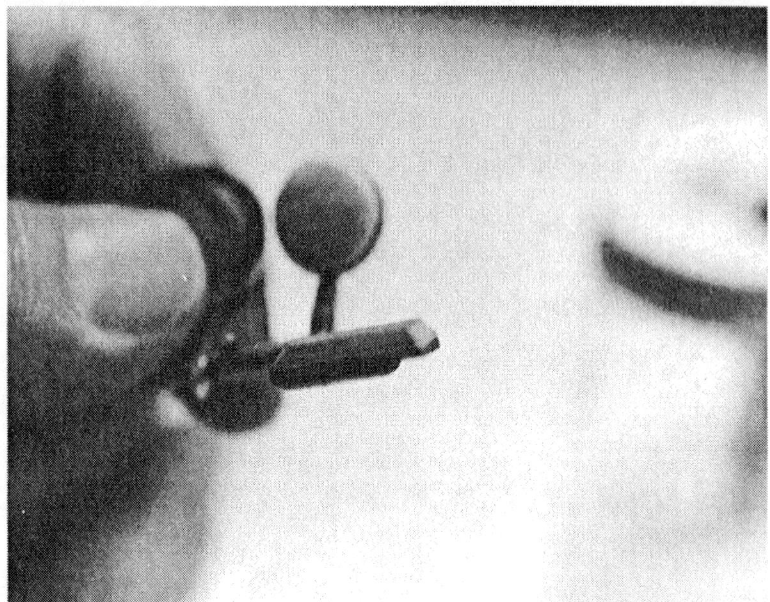

Photo 60. Tapered Cork

The distance a key opens is important to tone quality, pitch and technical evenness in the fingering of the instrument. Theorectically, the size of the tone hole determines the height of the key opening. This theory is true as far as minimum opening is concerned, but larger openings may be used with no detrimental effects, as evidenced by the height the fingers raise over the open holes in relation to the height of the key openings. For technical evenness we try to have all the keys on the top joint except the register key and thumb ring key open approximately the same distance.

The register key should open about 1/16-inch. If it opens further than this, the spatula (that part of a key touched in operation) should receive a thicker cork. If thicker cork raises the spatula too high for the player's thumb position, hold the pad cup closed and bend down on the spatula, curving the key to the point where the pad will open the correct distance. Most clarinets take 1/32-inch cork under the register spatula.

Third line Bb is probably the worst note, quality-wise, on the soprano clarinet. If this note sounds particularly bad, remove the register key and clean the register tube with a pipe cleaner or wood toothpick. Lint from the swab tends to collect here. If this does not clear up the problem, there are several different fingering combinations that will improve this note.

The key under the A spatula activated by both the thumb ring and the first finger ring (that I call the E ring key) also uses a small opening. The height of this opening is regulated by two corks, one under the thumb ring extension contacting the body of the clarinet and the other under the key lever that rides over this extension. Normally both of these corks are 1/64-inch thick. Should you need to lower the height of this key opening, put a thicker cork under the thumb ring extension. If you use a cork thicker than 1/64-inch between the two arms, the thumb extension will dig a groove in the cork where it contacts the upper arm. In time this groove will slow the action, sometimes even binding the keys. Often a piece of thin leather will give better action than cork between these arms. Due to the deep inset of this particular tone hole on some makes of clarinets the exact amount of the opening is difficult to judge. The real test is in the sound of the open G. If this G sounds free and clear, the key is opening far enough. If not, remove cork until the quality is clear.

The rest of the keys on the upper joint should open about 3/32-inch. Any that open much more than that should be recorked or bent back to correct shape.

Do not try to bend white metal or pot metal keys such as were used by Boosey-Hawkes and Conn Corp. during World War II on some of their student model instruments. They are almost sure to break. This type key cannot be silver-soldered as it will melt before it gets hot enough to make a weld. It is recognizable by a number cast on the underside.

For most people the rings should be level with the tops of the finger holes when depressed. If they are too high you must either use a thinner pad on the ring keys or bend the pad key arm in relation to the rings. It is better to change the pad than to bend the key, but if you feel that bending is necessary, block up the pad with a pad slick between the pad and the tone hole and press down on the rings. Press all rings concerned equally and at the same time. If the rings are too low, put in a thicker pad, put more cement in the cup or block up all rings concerned and bend down on the pad cup. Often a child with very small fingers has undue difficulty in getting the instrument to speak for him. The reason may be that the rings are too low. Raise the rings slightly above the tops of the finger holes to give small fingers more security in closing the ring keys.

Most clarinets are equipped with an adjusting screw to regulate the throat G# key. Be sure that there is 1/1000 or 2/1000-inch of play in the A key action before it contacts the G# key in order to insure proper closing of the G# tone hole. Any more play than this will feel awkward to the player. Where there is no regulating screw, the adjustment must be made with cork or leather. Do not use cork in conjunction with an adjusting screw as the screw will wear a hole in the cork in a very short time thus negating the adjustment. Use a dot of thin leather such as used on saxophone pads if you feel you must cushion the metal to metal contact.

Due to carelessness in handling, the bridge keys connecting the upper and lower ring keys are more often out of adjustment than any of the other keys. If they are bent, straighten them slowly and carefully and recork the bottom of the upper bridge. Assemble the two sections and check the Bb ring key on the lower joint and the Eb ring key on the upper joint. There should be equal drag on both keys. If this drag is unequal, fix it by bending either of the bridges. Tip the ends of the bridges up or down to adjust rather than trying to bend the arms in relation to the hinge. Regulate with thicker or thinner cork if necessary, but a cork on the bridge that is more than 1/32-inch thick will feel spongy.

As the tone holes get larger toward the bottom of the instrument, the pad openings should be greater. The chromatic B and the ring Bb keys should open about 3/32-inch, the same as the top joint keys. The remaining four larger pads should open about 1/8-inch or no more than 5/32-inch. This distance is measured at the front of the pad away from the hinge.

The most difficult adjustments on the clarinet involve the four right hand little finger keys. Because the G# key is independent of the other three, there is no real problem here. There should be a thin cork, either 1/64-inch or no thicker than 1/32-inch under the spatula to regulate the pad opening and quiet the action. On some clarinets the stop for this key is very small and soon digs a hole in the cork. A dot of thin leather held to the cork with Duco cement will correct this. If the pad opening is more than 5/32-inch after corking, hold the key cup closed and bend the spatula down until the correct height opening is achieved.

Using the same thickness pads with approximately the same amount of cement on each is the first step toward proper regulation of the last three keys. The F# key opening is controlled by the closing of the F key. Use 1/64-inch cork on the crow foot. Make sure the crow foot is level with the bottoms of the F# and the E spatula (Photos 61 and 62).

With the crow foot straight, parallel and corked, the F# key should open about 1/8-inch. If the opening is too great, hold the pad cup closed and bend the spatula down. If the opening is too small, bend the spatula up. Keep in mind that you cannot bend white metal keys without breaking them. The F# and F keys should now be opening the same distance and acting as stops for each other.

The F and E keys must both close when the E spatula is depressed. This is almost impossible to judge by eye, but a very accurate adjustment may be made with the feeler gauge. If the E is closing tightly and the F is loose, block the E pad up off the tone hole with a pad slick and bend down on the

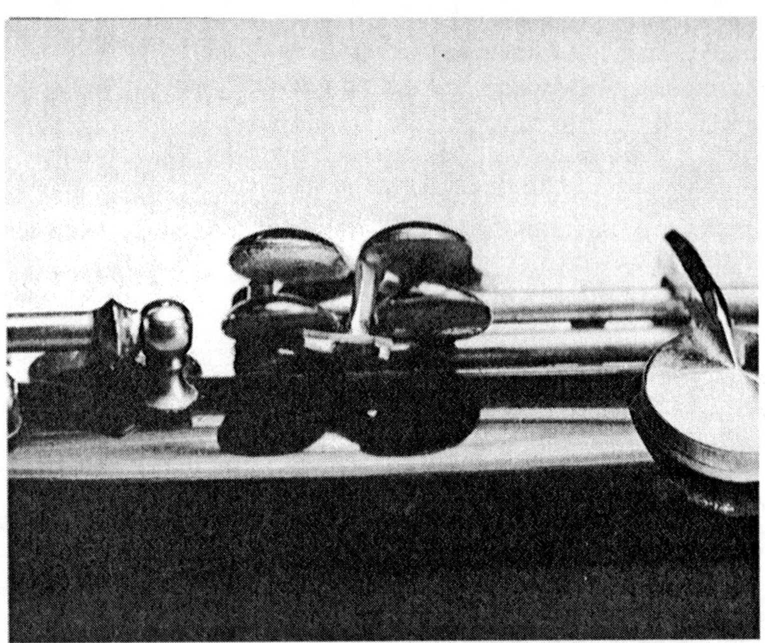

Photo 61. Straighten–Bend Crow Foot Level

Photo 62. Straighten–Bend Crow Foot Parallel to Keys

E spatula, changing the relationship of the cup to the spatula. If the F is closing tightly and the E is loose, hold the E pad cup closed and bend up on the E spatula. Sometimes the key metal is so strong and has so much spring that it is necessary to block a key higher than the thickness of the pad slick in order to bend a key. Remember that unless a key has been bent previously, it should not need bending to adjust. Check carefully to make sure the pads are the same depth in the pad cups before bending a key. Bend only when absolutely necessary. Dots of thin leather may be used to advantage on top of the crow foot cork to add thickness, or the cork may be sanded thinner to help with this adjustment. It is essential that these two pads hit with the same degree of tightness.

After regulating the E and F keys, we must remove all lost motion from them as follows:

When the F key crow foot fails to contact either the F# or the E spatulas, the cork on the back extension that contacts the left hand F lever is too thick. The F key opening will be too small (Photo 63).

Photo 63. Cork Too Thick on F Extension to Left Hand F

When the E spatula moves before contacting the crow foot, add cork to the bottom of the left hand E lever where it contacts the body of the clarinet. If there is already a 1/16-inch cork under this key, hold the E spatula down and hit the cross arm that connects to the left hand lever a sharp blow with a rawhide mallet, changing the angle between the cross arm and the spatula. The E key opening will be too large (Photo 64).

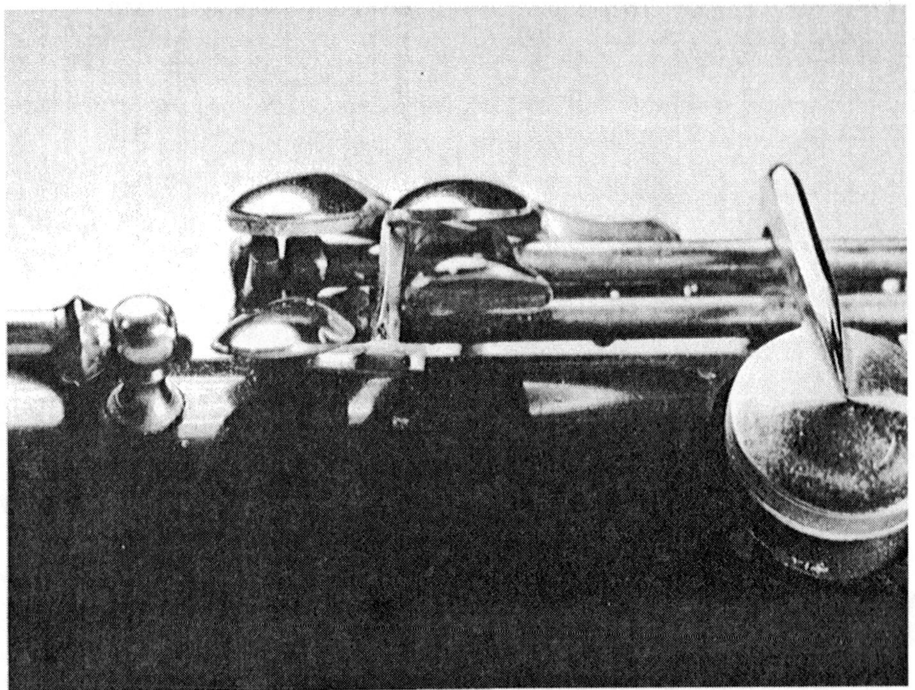

Photo 64. Add Cork to Bottom of Left Hand E Lever

If the lost motion is in the F# key, as in Photo 65, the F# key will be opening too far and the F# spatula should be bent down as described earlier. If the F# is not opening too far the angle of the cross arm on the key is too small or the cork under the left hand E is too thick. The E key opening will be too small.

Photo 65. Bend F# Spatula Down

It is vitally important that you study every situation for a moment until you can figure out why a key acts in a certain way. When you have this figured out, chances are that you can correct the problem.

The left hand E and F# keys should have a thickness of fish skin over the pin that inserts into the hole in the cross arms (Photo 66). This is about a 1/4-inch circle or square that may be cut from a discarded pad or purchased very reasonably by the hundred. On this type clarinet there is usually a 1/16-inch cork on the bottom of the E lever and no

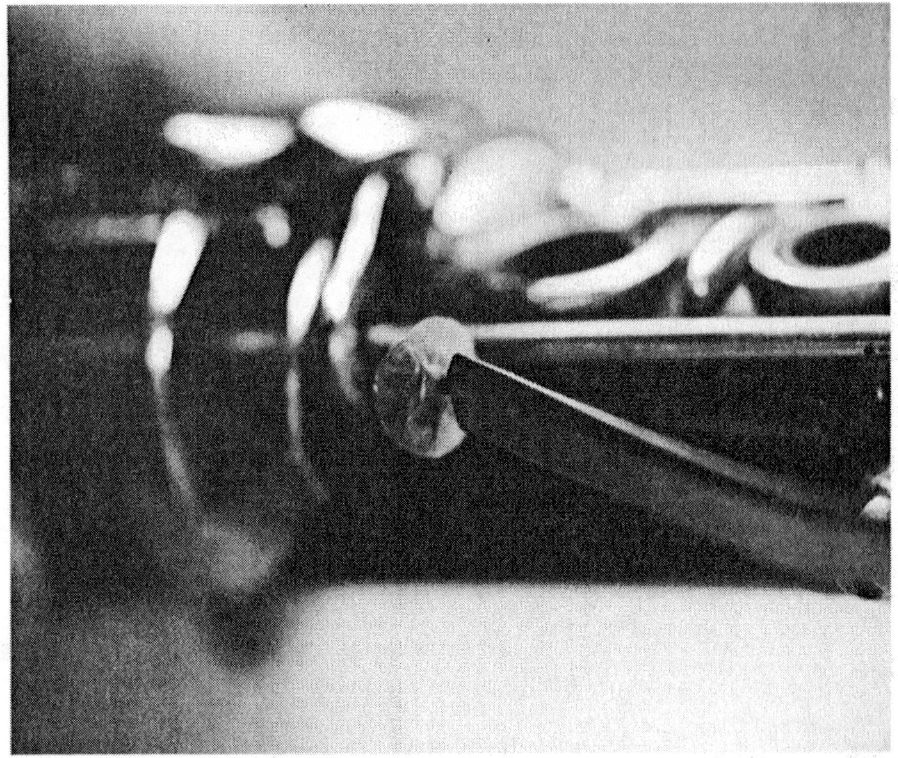

Photo 66. Position Fish Skin Silencer

cork on the F#. When the left hand levers form a ledge to contact the cross arms, there should be a 1/64-inch cork under the cross arms where contact is made with the ledge. On this type you must remove the lost motion from the left hand F# lever with a cork on the bottom. Be careful not to make this too thick as it will hold the F# key open. Allow only 1/1000 or 2/1000-inch of play (Photo 67).

Some repair technicians use a leak light on clarinets and flutes. Because the bladder pad is so translucent, I prefer to use a feeler gauge. If you have the money to purchase a leak light, do so by all means as it is essential for saxophones even if you decide not to use it on clarinets and flutes.

Photo 67. Right Hand Little Finger Keys
in Correct Alignment

Repair Notes

9

REPLACING FLUTE PADS

The C key and the trill key pads on flute are replaced in the same manner as clarinet pads. The most minute leak in any of these three pads will cause trouble down the entire range of the instrument, so check these pads first if a student is experiencing difficulty. Any break in the skin or any variation in tightness detected with the feeler gauge should be remedied.

The remainder of the flute pads are held in place with a screw and washer or a plastic snap, and in the case of an open hole flute, with a metal grommet.

The key needing the new pad must be removed from the instrument. Before taking the worn pad out of the cup, note the approximate distance the pad protrudes from the cup. This distance varies with different makes, some being nearly level with the rim while others protrude up to 1/32-inch out of the cup.

Select a pad that fills the cup as tightly as possible without distorting the flat surface of the skin and felt. Make sure that the hole in the pad is large enough to allow the pad to sit clear down in the cup. Some makes of flute have such a large flange on the nut soldered in the center of the cup that it is necessary to cut out some of the cardboard on the back of the pad in order to allow the pad to fit down tightly.

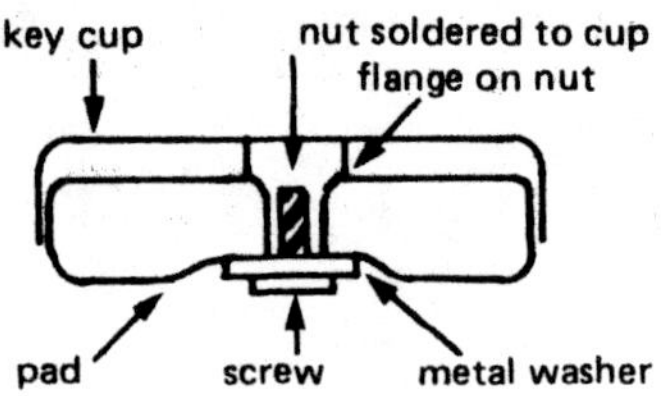

Figure 2.

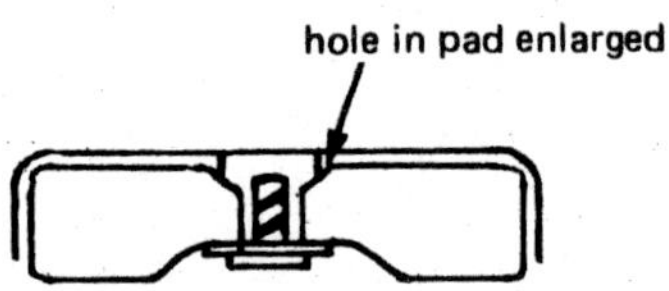

Figure 3.

In Figure 2 the hole in the pad is too small. You would have to fill in the bottom of the cup with a number of paper washers to keep the pad from rocking. Chances are this would make the pad too thick, extending too far above the cup rim and thus hitting the tone hole in the back near the hinge. Figure 3 shows the same pad with the center hole enlarged in the cardboard allowing it to fit down over the flange on the nut and rest securely on the bottom of the cup, or on one or two paper washers as needed. Secure the pad in the cup with the screw and washer. In tightening the screw, the washer will tend to turn clockwise thus raising wrinkles in the skin on the pad. These wrinkles may be smoothed with a flute pad iron warmed over your lamp and applied to the pad with a semi-circular motion, or at this stage they may be ignored without serious consequence.

Replace the key on the flute and check the new pad with the feeler gauge. Be sure to loosen any adjusting screw or remove any cork that may be holding the pad from making contact with the tone hole. If the pad is tight to the tone hole in front but loose in the back at the hinge, you must remove the pad and insert a paper washer or two in the cup to make the pad thicker. When the pad hits tightly in back and is loose in front, it is too thick, and must be lowered further into the cup. Remove a washer or two if any were used. If no washers were used, check to make sure the hole in the pad is large enough to fit down over the flange on the nut as described earlier. If the pad still hits in back and is down tightly into the bottom of the cup it is too thick for the instrument. In this case, you will have to tilt the pad in the cup by using a partial washer in the front of the cup. Both sides will test the same unless the pad cup has been bent. If the cup tilts sideways, straighten it by placing your pad slick between the cup and the tone hole rim on the low side and press down with your finger on the high side.

In selecting the paper washers make sure the washer is large enough to completely cover the cup from edge to edge. A washer too small that manages to shift a bit off center may fail to support the pad edge as needed. Many repairmen use a washer that is too large for the cup, cutting a small pie-shaped wedge from it allowing it to be sprung into the cup with the assurance that it will fill the cup tightly to the walls. It is good policy to mark the pad with a pencil line pointing to the center of the hinge arm so that in this trial and error method of determining the exact thickness of washers needed you can replace the pad in the same position every time.

It is my own personal opinion that partial washers are necessary only in the front of the cup, and then very seldom, as the back should be raised with full washers and the sides leveled by aligning the cup. Be very careful to use no pressure in closing the key during testing with the feeler. A little too much pressure can make a poorly leveled pad feel quite satisfactory. There should be a slightly tighter feeling at the back of the pad than at the front to allow for perfect seating after the pad has been wet and tied down as this process actually makes the pad thinner where it contacts the tone hole rim.

To seat the new pad, wet it with a moistened pipe cleaner or small water color brush and tie the key closed with a strip of cloth or clamp it with a flute key clamp. Allow no water to reach the hinge, as this will rust the steel hinge pin and raise havoc with the key action. It is good policy to hold the flute in such a manner while wetting the pad that any excess water will drop down away from the hinge. Leave the key tied or clamped closed overnight.

When perfectly dry, you must regulate the new pad key to work correctly in combination with the other keys as intended.

Any pad where the skin is broken in past the tone hole seat will leak and should be changed. As with clarinet pads, good quality flute pads are double skin, and it is possible for the top skin to be broken with the bottom skin still intact. This should still be sealing and need not be changed. A magnifying glass or jeweler's loupe is a big help in checking, as it is sometimes difficult to determine whether the bottom skin or the felt is exposed.

10

REGULATING THE FLUTE

The first step in regulating the flute is to make sure the head joint cork is properly positioned and is airtight. Insert the cleaning rod in the open end of the joint and see that the tuning mark on the rod lines up in the exact center of the blow hole. Place the cleaning rod in contact with the plate on the tuning cork. If the tuning mark is down the flute from the center, tighten the crown to pull the cork further up the head. When the line is above center, loosen the crown and push the cork down the joint until the tuning mark is centered (Photo 68).

If this cork moves easily you should be suspicious of a leak. Check it for leakage by holding your finger over the blow hole and sucking the air from the head joint. You should get a good vacuum, and the head joint should stick to your lips for almost thirty seconds as shown in Photo 69. If you cannot get this vacuum, the leak must be stopped.

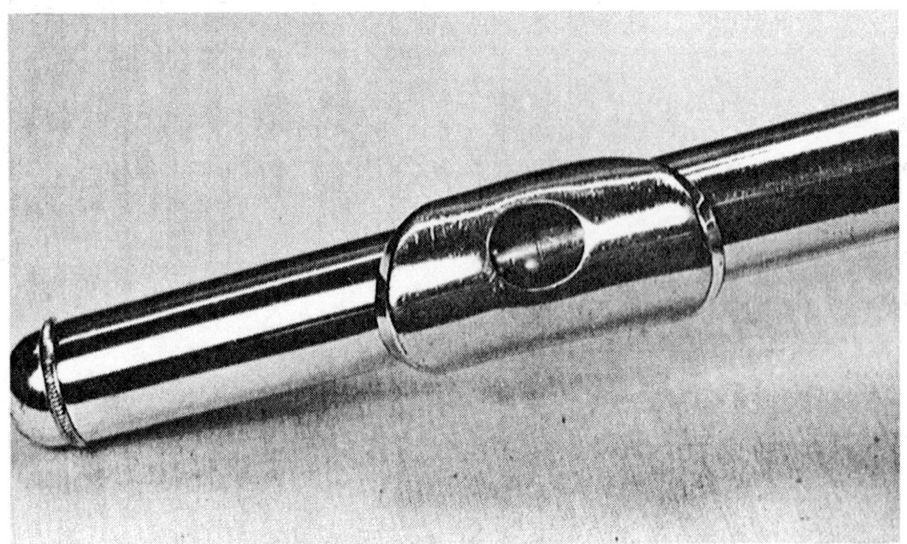

Photo 68. Head Joint Cork Correctly Positioned

Photo 69. Good Vacuum in Head Joint

Remove the crown and push the cork out the opposite end. The flute head joint is slightly tapered and parabolic in shape with the closed crown end smaller than the open tenon to the body, so the cork must be pushed down the joint to the larger end. When the cork is corroded and does not move easily, there is less chance of damaging the cork assembly if you use a 5/8-inch dowel about 8-inches long and a rawhide mallet rather than trying to push on the cork assembly with the cleaning rod. Drill a 3/16-inch hole in the center of the dowel about 1-inch deep so that force will be applied to the metal disc rather than the threaded rod which can be easily bent (Photo 70). Hold the head joint and dowel in the air when tapping with the mallet as shown in Photo 71. Never tap with the joint supported on the bench. If the cork is broken to any great extent it should be replaced. When it is still good, but just too compressed, clean it carefully and wrap it with a layer or two of Scotch Magic Tape. This plastic tape will last as long as the cork.

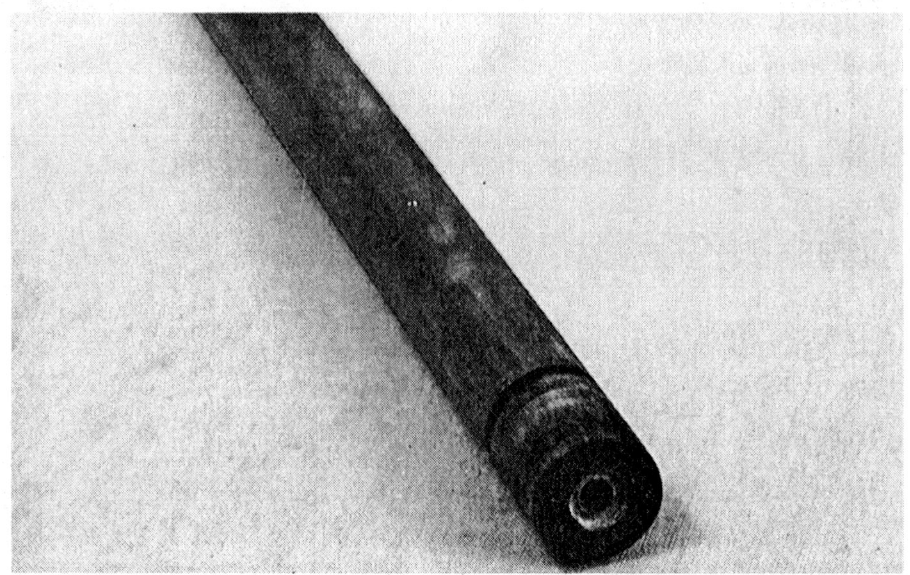

Photo 70. Dowel Drilled to Remove Head Cork Assembly

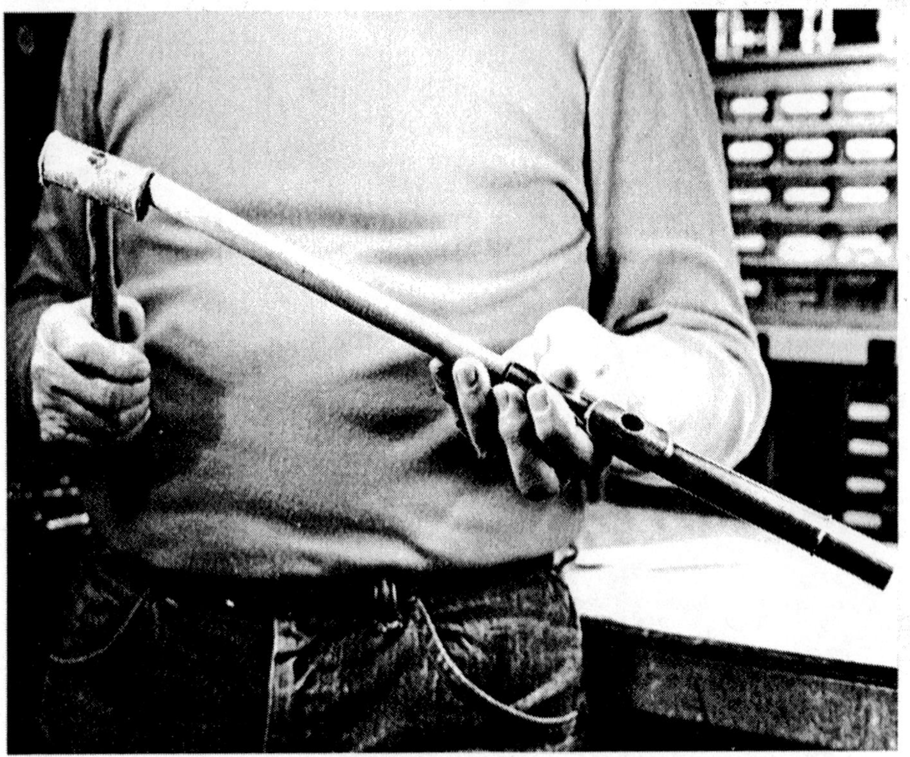

Photo 71. Removing Head Cork Assembly

Wash the open head joint, grease the cork and replace it, screw first, from the bottom of the joint (Photo 72). Again, it is better to use the dowel than to try to push it in place with the cleaning rod. Test for vacuum again. If the cork is tight and you still get air leaks, there is a break in the solder holding the embouchure plate. This should be resoldered by a repair technician.

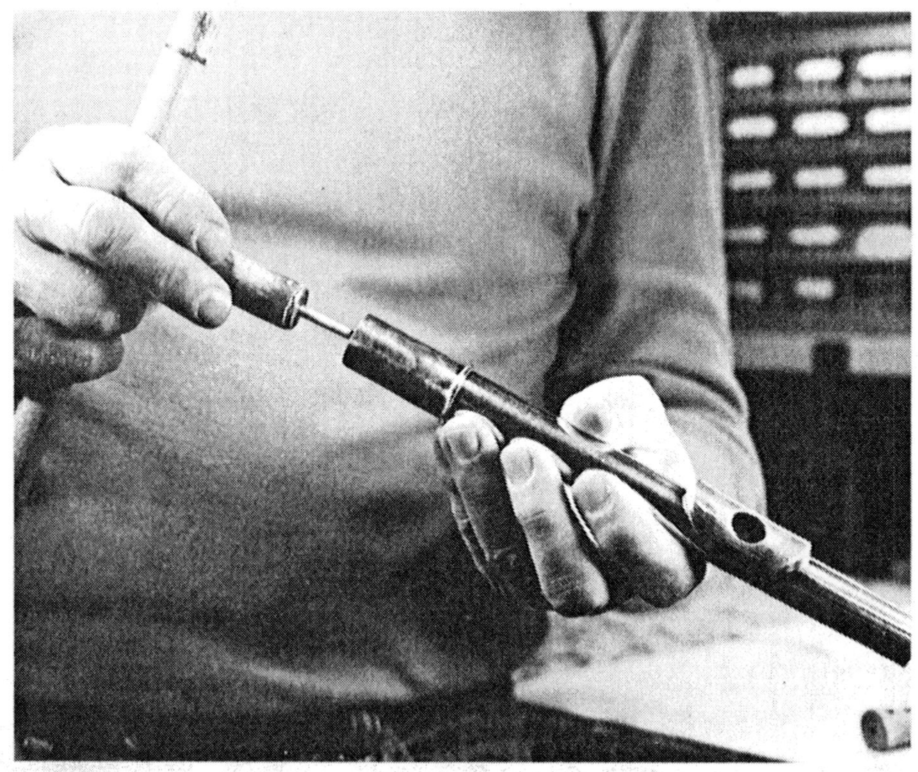

Photo 72. Replacing Head Cork Assembly

Make all testings for regulation by using the feeler gauge. It is next to impossible to sight the necessary adjustments. The first adjustment should be the F–Bb bridge. Loosen the adjusting screw that regulates the F# key from the F to enable you to accurately gauge the F to Bb. This adjustment is made in the bridge connecting the right and left hand stacks. There should be a 1/64-inch cork on the bottom of the upper bridge. Check this first. If the cork is satisfactory, and the long screw C key hinge is in tightly but the Bb key still does not close with the F, tip the upper bridge down slightly with your round-nose pliers as shown in Photo 73. Tip the bottom bridge up slightly to make them parallel. A regulation will not last long unless both bridges are in full contact with each other. If the Bb key closes too tightly thus holding the F key open, bend the bottom bridge down and the top bridge up.

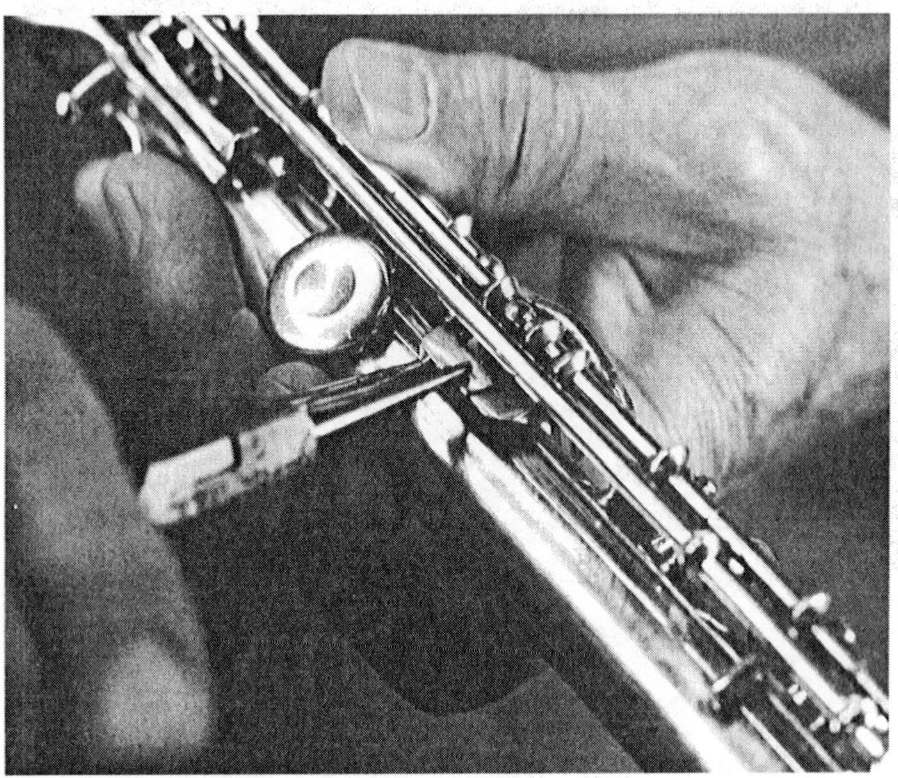

Photo 73. Regulating Bridge

Before doing any bending on this bridge be sure there is no play in the pivot hinges of either right or left hand stacks because if there is, no amount of regulation will be satisfactory. If all hinge screws are tight and there is still play in the stacks, take the flute to a repair shop. Check, too, for any play in the Bb key itself on the upper stack. This might be caused by just a loose stack pin which you can tighten by removing the stack. Support the key from the bottom on the corner of a wood or lead block and drive the pin in with your bench hammer (Photo 74). If light tapping fails to remove the play, take it to a shop where an oversize pin will have to be fitted to make up for wear or stretch in the soft key metal of the outer hinge.

Photo 74. Tightening Loose Hinge Pin

After the F to Bb bridge is regulated, regulate the F# to the F with the adjusting screw. Do not be satisfied until the F, F# and Bb all feel exactly the same to your gauge. When these are exact, regulate the E to F# and then the D to F#. At this point we are concerned with the closing of the pads. Do not worry if some open higher than others and have motion before contacting another key. We will take care of this problem later.

With the right hand stack and the bridge regulated, the next step is the A to Bb in the left hand. Do this with the adjusting screw on the A key in the same manner in which you regulated the right hand stack. If any of these adjusting screws seem very free or loose, clean the top of the screw and the edge of the threaded hole with a Q-tip cotton swab and alcohol, and put a drop of Duco cement or clear nail polish on them to help hold the adjustment you have just made.

The final regulation on the main body is to adjust the thumb Bb lever to close the thumb B key and the Bb key simultaneously. If the cork on the Bb key arm (Photo 75) is worn thin or is missing, replace it with 1/64-inch cork. The adjustment will not hold in thicker cork. Do not attempt to bend this arm unless you know exactly what you are doing. Bending pressure used on any key pinned to its hinge with a tapered pin as is the case here, and in the right hand stack to the F# key, will usually enlarge the pin hole in the soft key metal of the outer hinge instead of bending the key as you intended. This then becomes a costly major repair.

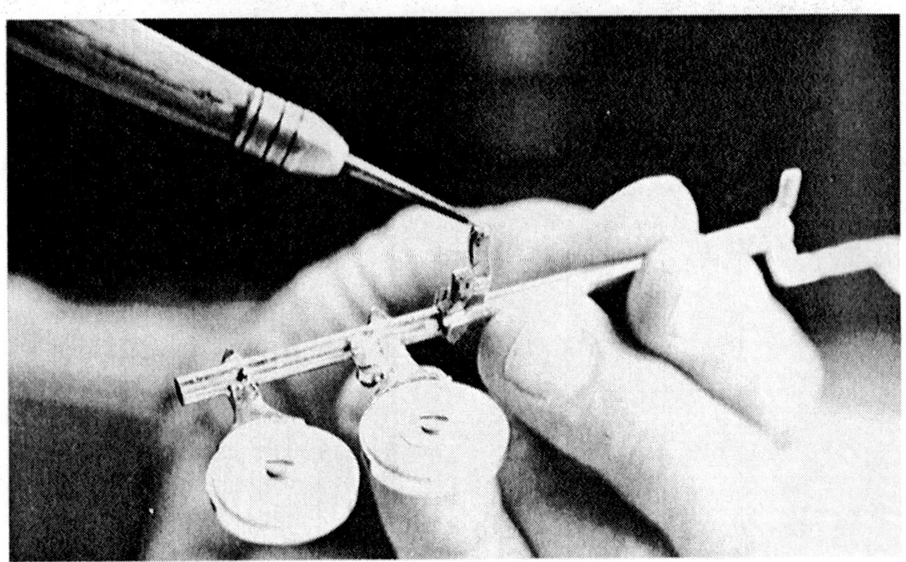

Photo 75. Bb Key Arm

When the thumb B key closes before the Bb key and the cork on the Bb arm is satisfactory, the felt or cork on the Bb lever directly over the thumb B key must be made thinner. If the Bb key closes before the thumb B key, add thickness to the felt or cork on this same lever. A combination of correct thickness cork is needed on both the Bb arm and the thumb Bb lever (Photo 75A). This lever may be bent up or down slightly to assist the corks with the regulation.

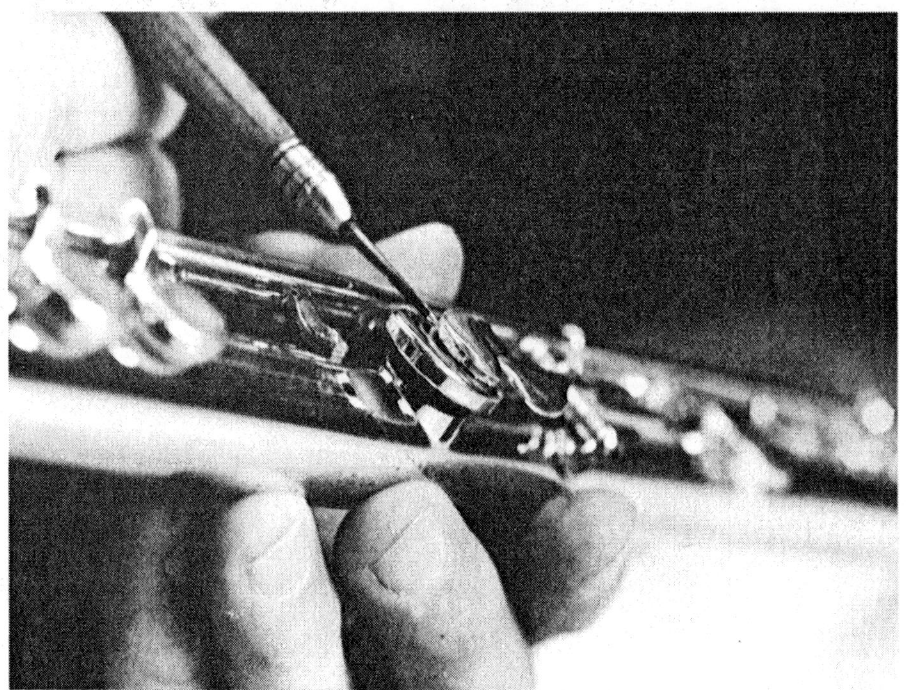

Photo 75A. Cork on Thumb Bb Key Lever

The foot joint is often out of adjustment. Usually the problem is that the C# key fails to close when the C roller is pressed. Here again the cork between the C and C# is usually either missing or compressed. Remove the keys, put a new piece of 1/64-inch cork between the keys and check again. If the C# still does not close, hold the C# key cup closed with your thumb and bend up on the C# spatula with flat-nose pliers as shown in Photo 76. Bend this spatula up until the C and C# keys feel exactly the same to your gauge when when the low C roller is depressed.

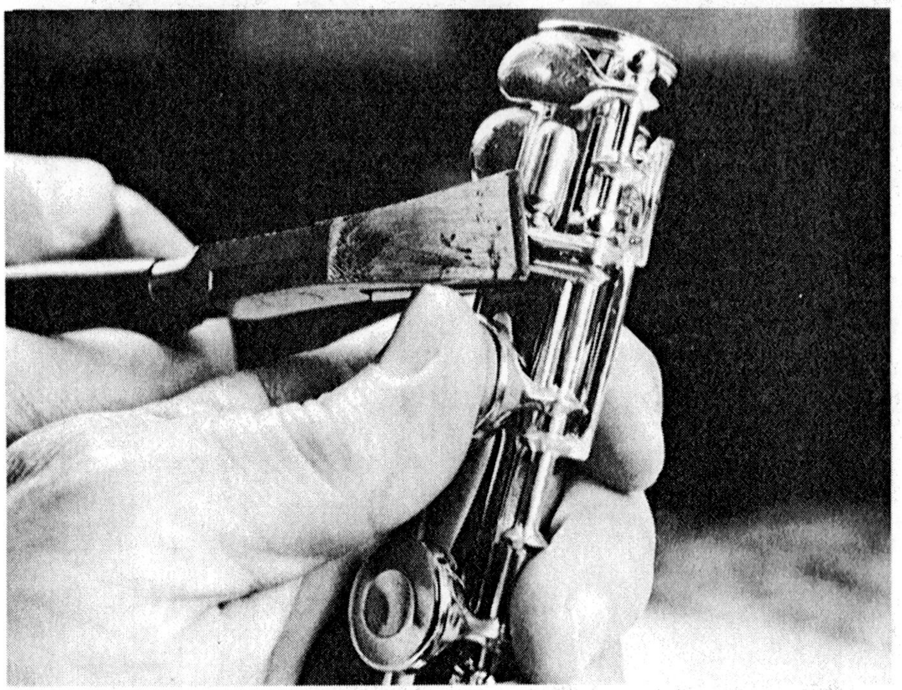

Photo 76. Regulating C# Key

Up to this point we have been concerned only with the correct closing of the pads. The correct height opening is also important. Starting again with the F–Bb bridge, check these keys for correct height when open. If they open much more than 1/8-inch, add cork to the bottom of the right-hand bridge. If they do not open far enough, remove some of the cork from here. Too thick a cork on the A foot will keep the Bb and the A keys from opening the correct distance. The same condition on either the E or the D feet will keep the F, F# and Bb from opening far enough.

Your problem is more likely to be with keys that open too far resulting in lost motion in a key before it contacts the lug that closes its companion key. This is caused by a missing foot cork or a cork compressed by wear. In the case of a compressed cork and a tiny bit of lost motion, a small dot of saxophone pad leather cemented to the cork with Duco cement will often correct the situation. If the cork is missing, remove the key and recork as described in Chapter 9. There should be absolutely no lost motion in any of the keys.

The height of the key openings on the foot joint should be slightly more than 1/8-inch and is regulated by the thickness of cork on the foot of the C key. If there is already a 1/16-inch cork on the C key foot and it still opens too far, the foot has been bent up and needs only to be bent back down. The trill keys and the left hand C key should not open quite as far as the rest of the main body keys.

Should you lose one of the three extra thick corks from the trill keys or the low Eb key, a replacement may be made from a bottle cork.

Repair Notes

11

PISTON VALVE BRASS

With brass instruments, the focus of attention for the instrumental music teacher should be on preventative maintenance rather than on actual repair. A great majority of all brass repair work taken into a shop could be prevented by proper instruction on the part of the teacher.

Do not be overly concerned about small dents. Dents less than 1/4 of the diameter of the tubing have little effect on the playing qualities of the instrument (Photo 77). A dent in the mouthpipe that is deeper than 1/4 of the diameter may change the feel of the way the instrument blows and should be sent to a shop for removal (Photo 78). Dents in the bell and bell throat have to be quite bad to damage anything except the looks of the instrument and peace of mind of the owner.

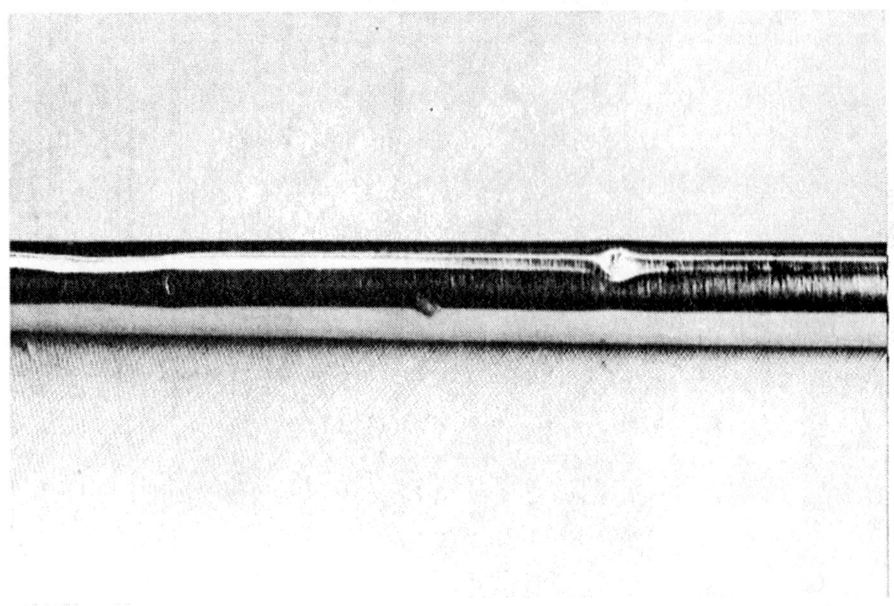

Photo 77. Trumpet Mouthpipe Small Dents

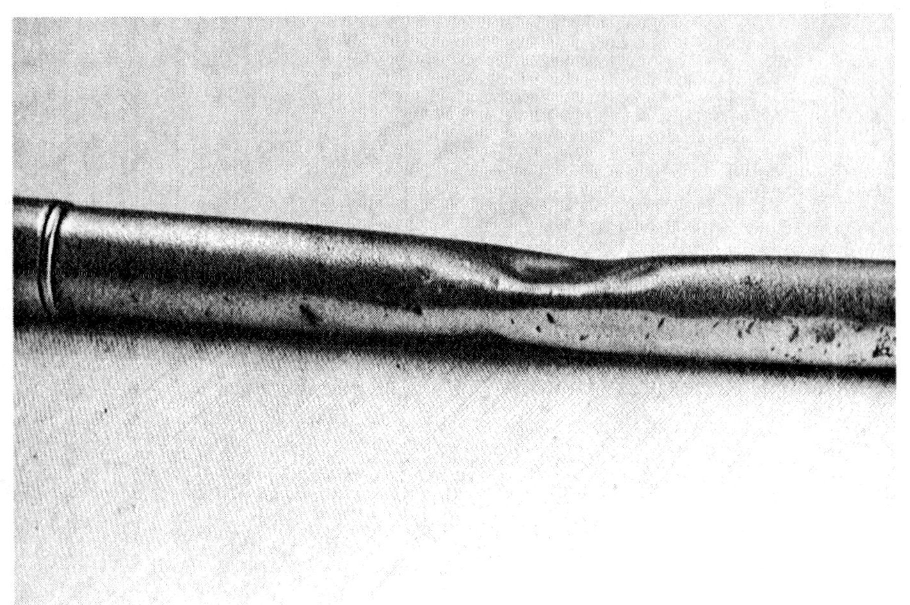

Photo 78. This Mouthpipe Dent Should Be Removed

Stuck slides and mouthpieces are probably the initial cause of eighty percent of brass instrument damage. It is within your province to greatly minimize such damage.

You or your school should own two basic brass repair tools, namely the Ferree's mouthpiece puller,[1] and a tapered punch or the Mero Products mouthpiece tool. A mouthpiece will become frozen over a period of time by corrosion if not removed regularly. Teach your students to remove the mouthpiece every time and store it in a location in the case where it cannot bounce around to dent the instrument. A stuck mouthpiece most commonly occurs, however, when the mouthpiece is dropped, causing a flat area on the end of the shank as shown in Photo 79. Usually you can re-round the shank with Mero's tapered tool and ordinary hand pressure (Photo 79A). If the end of the shank is very thick, as is sometimes the case with tuba and baritone mouthpieces, you may have to use a small hammer in conjunction with the tapered tool and perhaps even a fine file (Photo 80).

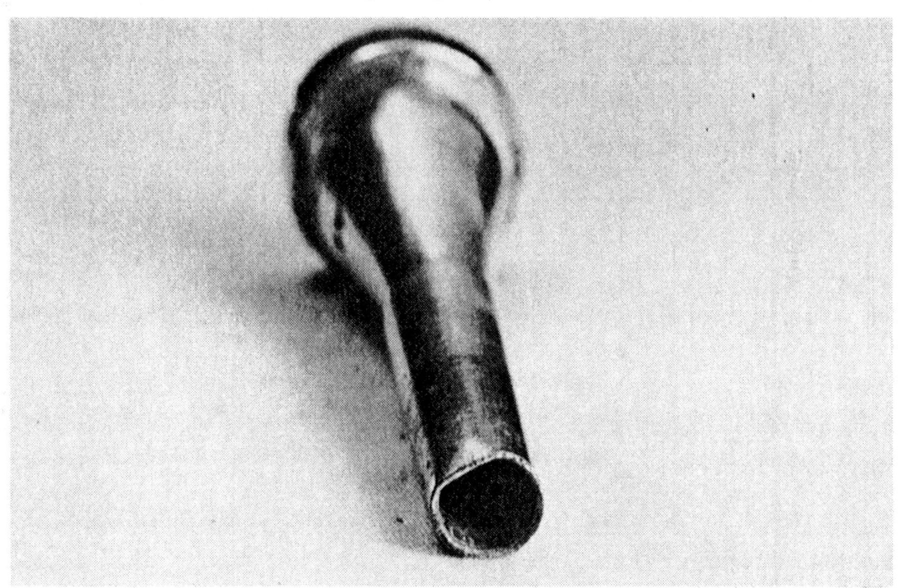

Photo 79. Prelude to a Stuck Mouthpiece

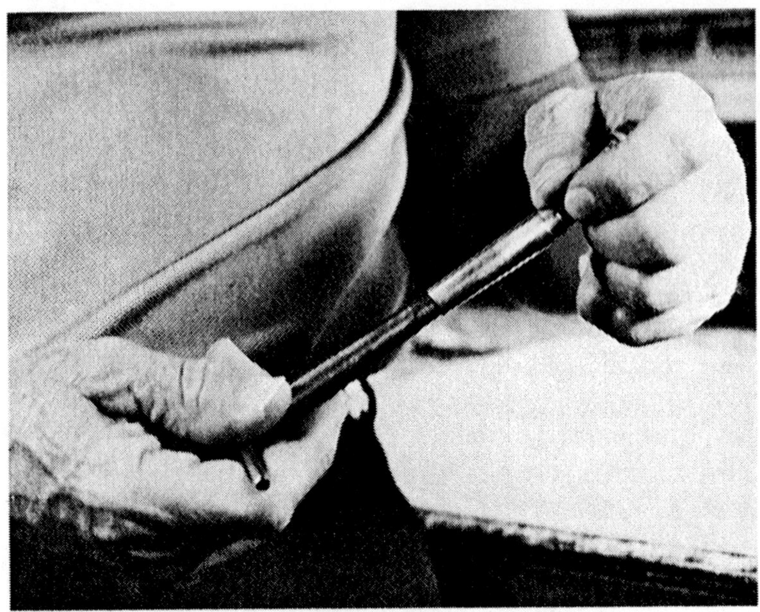

Photo 79A. Rerounding Mouthpiece Shank

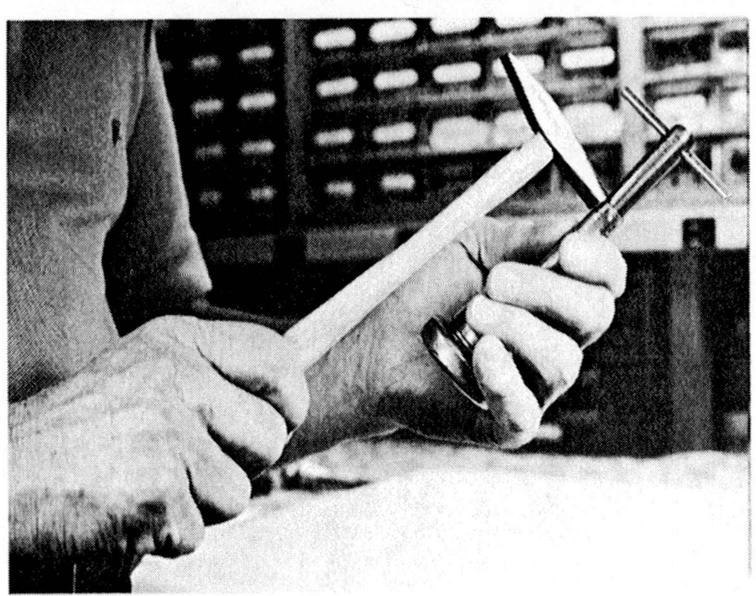

Photo 80. Rerounding Heavy Shank

If filing is necessary, you will remove the silver plating as you file. This is not harmful to the mouthpiece except in appearance. It is much more important that the mouthpiece taper fits the receiver perfectly than that the mouthpiece looks good. You should, however, warn a student away from a mouthpiece where the plating is worn through on the rim, as brass in contact with the lips is very apt to cause infection.

Ferree's mouthpiece puller will remove the most stubborn of stuck mouthpieces, and it fits all sizes from horn through giant tuba with the same saddle and no extra pieces to change or misplace (Photo 81).

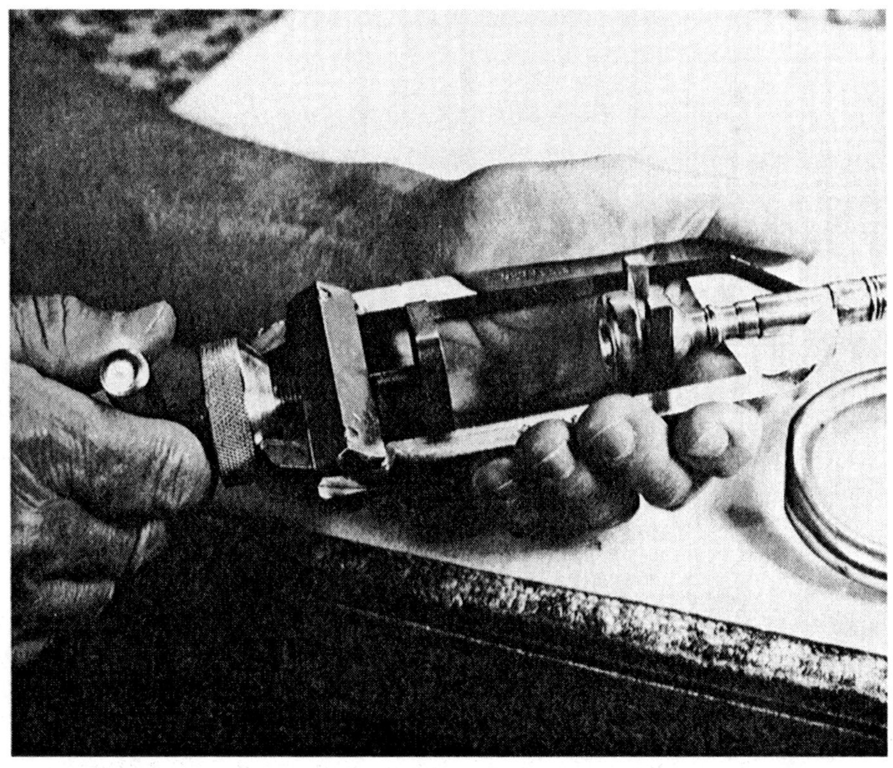

Photo 81. Removing Stuck Mouthpiece with Ferree's Puller

Be sure to inform your students that you have a puller and will remove a stuck mouthpiece for them. If you fail to tell them, they will invariably have a well-intentioned father try to remove it, and if firmly stuck, the end result is often a twisted mouthpipe, broken braces, a vise or plier-damaged mouthpiece or a combination of all three of these undesirables necessitating a costly trip to a repair shop.

Examine your students' mouthpieces periodically. The most critical spot in the entire instrument is the throat of the mouthpiece. Do not tolerate a dirty mouthpiece, as it affects both tone quality and pitch—to say nothing of the germs it harbors. Should there be a buildup that will not wash out, immerse the mouthpiece for a few seconds in a 50/50 solution of muriatic acid and water, then wash it with soap and water using a mouthpiece brush or pipe cleaner. Sometimes the acid will tarnish the silver plating, but that can be readily removed with silver polish.

The second most critical area is the mouthpipe. Keep it clean with a snake-type brush, warm water and a mild detergent. Contrary to some beliefs, detergent will not harm modern lacquers if rinsed promptly with warm water and wiped dry with a clean, soft cloth.

Valves and slides should be removed and the inside of the entire instrument washed and flushed regularly. The frequency of this washing is arbitrary, and depends upon the number of hours a day the instrument is used, and the care a student takes in rinsing his mouth when the instrument is used shortly after meals, snacking, or soft drinks. I suggest that such a cleaning once a month would keep most instruments relatively clean inside.

Although not as critical with a tuba as with a French horn or cornet because of the larger bore, it is also very important to keep the larger horns clean on the inside. When weather permits, take the basses outdoors on the grass, remove valves and slides to a plastic dishpan filled with warm water and detergent. Then, with a trombone snake-brush, scrub the mouthpipe, each slide and each tube as far as the brush will reach. After that flush with a garden hose from which the metal nozzle connector has been removed. Lubricate, reassemble and wipe the outside clean and dry with a soft cloth. In the wintertime take them into the shower room and use the same procedure. Basses are usually very dirty and corroded inside because this vital periodic flushing is neglected.

Great care must be exercised by you, the teacher, when giving instruction in this brushing and flushing process because careless or very young students can do serious damage to valves and slides by dropping them or banging them against a sink or basin.

Proper cleaning is impossible if any of the slides are stuck. It is your responsibility to explain the importance of well lubricated slides. Over the years I have used a variety of lubricants from Vaseline to bearing grease, to hydrous wool fat lanolin, and finally to Shell's STP oil treatment on a tip from a student in one of my classes. I find the STP far superior to any of the other slide lubricants. This, of course, is too heavy to use on a slide where a trigger mechanism or finger ring is employed to bring down the pitch.

There are several reasons why a slide becomes stuck. Probably the most common is failing to use proper lubrication so the minerals in the saliva corrode the slide. A dent in the outer slide, and it need not be a deep one, will make it extremely difficult to remove, or if the instrument has been dropped or knocked, the slides may be pushed out of parallel. I suggest the following method to remove a stuck tuning slide. From a cardboard template made by tracing the inside radius of the frozen slide (Photo 82), make an implement of 3/4-inch soft wood as shown in Photo 83. File it or sand it until it fits the inside radius of the stuck slide perfectly. A few blows on this implement with a rawhide mallet will usually move the slide (Photo 84). Use discretion and good judgment and if the slide does not budge, send it to a repair shop before you

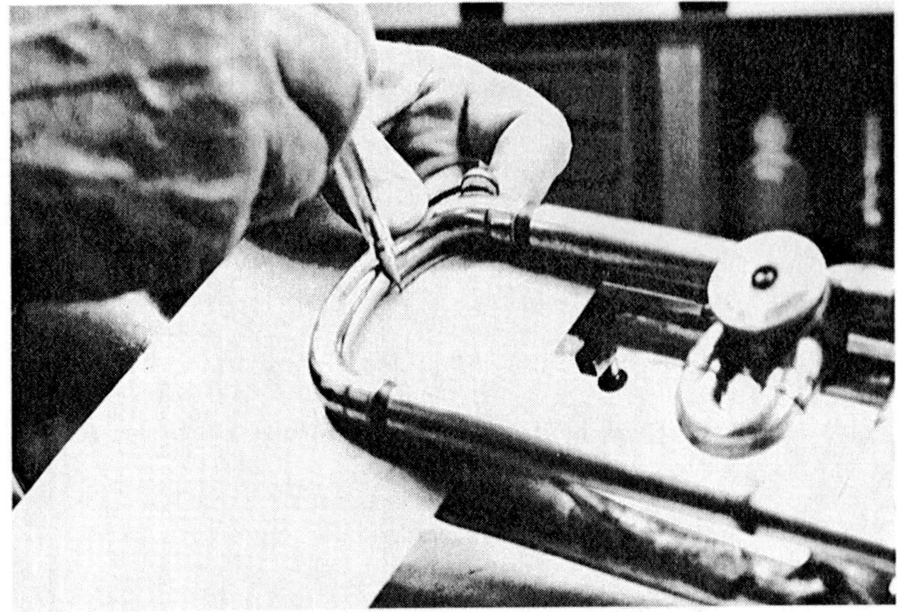

Photo 82. Making Template

Photo 83. Soft Wood Implement for Tuning Slide Removal

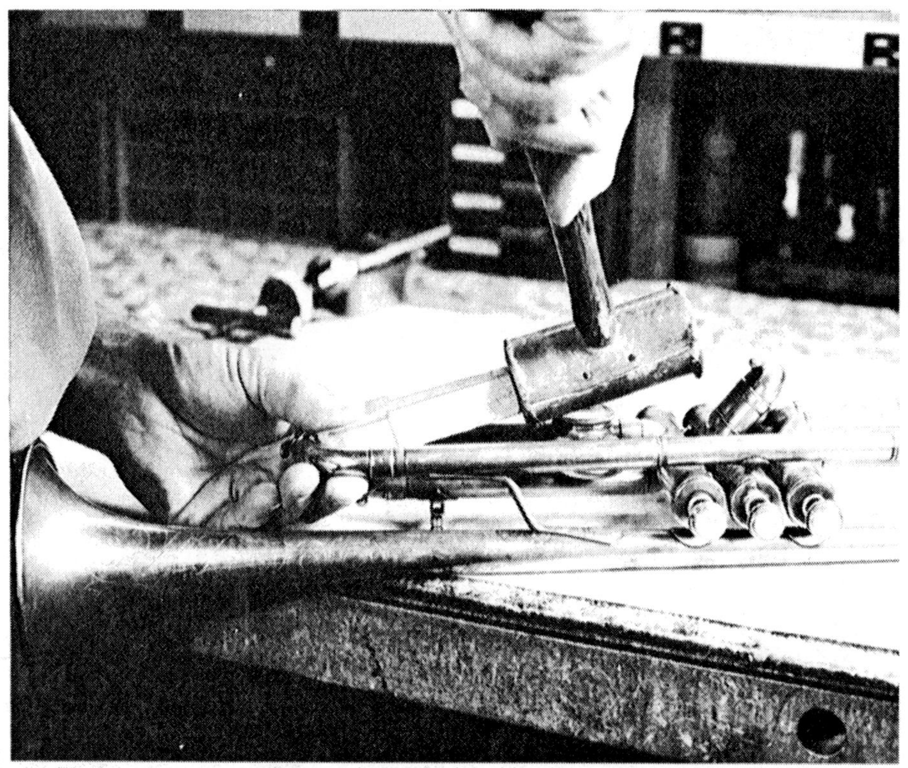

Photo 84. Removing Frozen Tuning Slide

bend or break any braces or knock the horn out of line. It is especially easy to drive a bow out of line when one side comes free and the other does not. The repairman will unsolder the bow and remove the slides one at a time. Using a rope or cloth will dent and pull the bow out of shape as well as break the braces if too much force is applied.

The valve slides can usually be removed by putting a tapered punch down into the bow until the outside radius of the taper reaches the size of the inside radius of the slide bow. Tap against the side of the punch with a rawhide mallet as shown in Photo 85. Sometimes a few drops of penetrating oil allowed to work overnight will help.

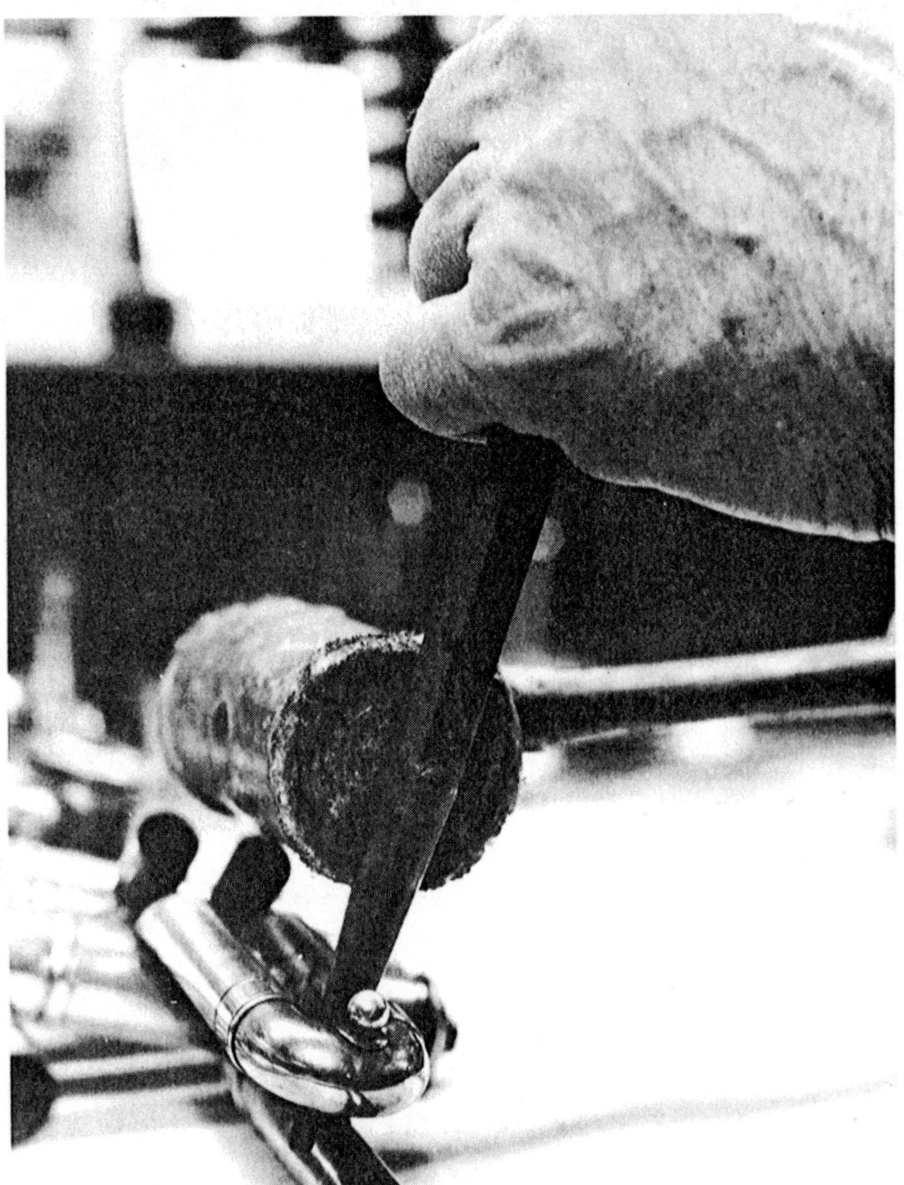

Photo 85. Removing Valve Slide with Tapered Punch

Once the slide is out, clean it by immersing it for a few seconds in the muriatic acid solution. Brush it thoroughly inside with a trumpet snake-brush, wash in detergent and rinse. Polish the unlacquered slides with 0000 steel wool. Lubricate with STP and work it in and out (each side separately) until free. If it fails to work freely with this treatment there is a dent in the slide or the slides have been bent out of parallel, in which case it should go into a shop to be straightened.

Take about two minutes at the beginning of every brass class to have your students move each slide in and out about 1/4-inch and turn both top and bottom valve caps a half turn and back. This quick and easy procedure will enable you to detect at a glance any slide that is stuck or in need of lubrication, and hopefully allow you to fix it before it becomes a repair shop problem.

How often have you asked a student to pull his tuning slide and heard, "I can't, it's stuck!"?

NOTES

1. Ferree's Band Instrument Tools and Supplies, 1477 E. Michigan, Battle Creek, Mich. 49016

Repair Notes

12

REGULATING PISTON VALVES

If a valve instrument is clean inside, has no cracks, deep dents or leaks and still responds poorly, chances are that the pistons need to be realigned. When the piston is correctly aligned, the ports in the piston coincide exactly with the ports in the casing.

To assist you in this vital regulation, most manufacturers have cut a groove around the valve stem that is level with the top of the valve cap when the alignment is correct on the up-stroke. Should the groove appear above the level, replace the felts as the old ones have become compressed through use. If the grooves are below level, the thickness of the felt and cork combination that contacts the bottom of the top valve cap is too great and should be replaced with material of the correct thickness.

Sometimes there is no mark on the valve stem, and once in a while they are marked incorrectly. To check this alignment make or buy a tool like that shown in Photo 86. It consists of: (1) a bar about 8 inches long, (2) a fairly heavy needle spring pressed into a drilled hole and extending about 1/4-inch, and (3) a slide with a bottom extension and a thumb screw to lock it in varying positions.

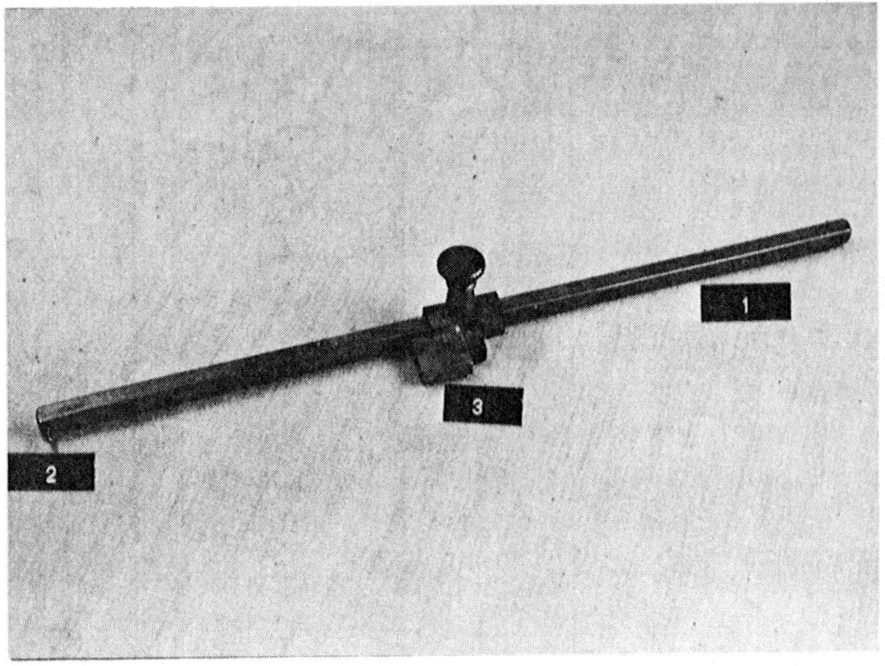

Photo 86. Tool for Aligning Piston Valves Up-Stroke

An old trombone lyre with an adjustable holder will furnish the necessary materials. Cut the bar to length, saw the lyre off from the slide, then soft-solder an extension on the slide level with the bottom of the slide and on the side opposite the thumb screw. This tool and the valve mirror mentioned later may be purchased from any band instrument repair tool company.

To use this tool, insert it into the second valve casing, catch the point (2) in the top of the port leading to the third valve casing, bring the slide down level touching the top of the casing and tighten the screw (Photo 87). Remove the tool from the casing and insert the point in the corresponding port in the second valve. When the point is tight against the top of the port, the distance from the top of the valve proper to the bottom of the tool slide previously positioned will give you the exact thickness of combined cork and felt required to align the ports on the up-stroke (Photo 88).

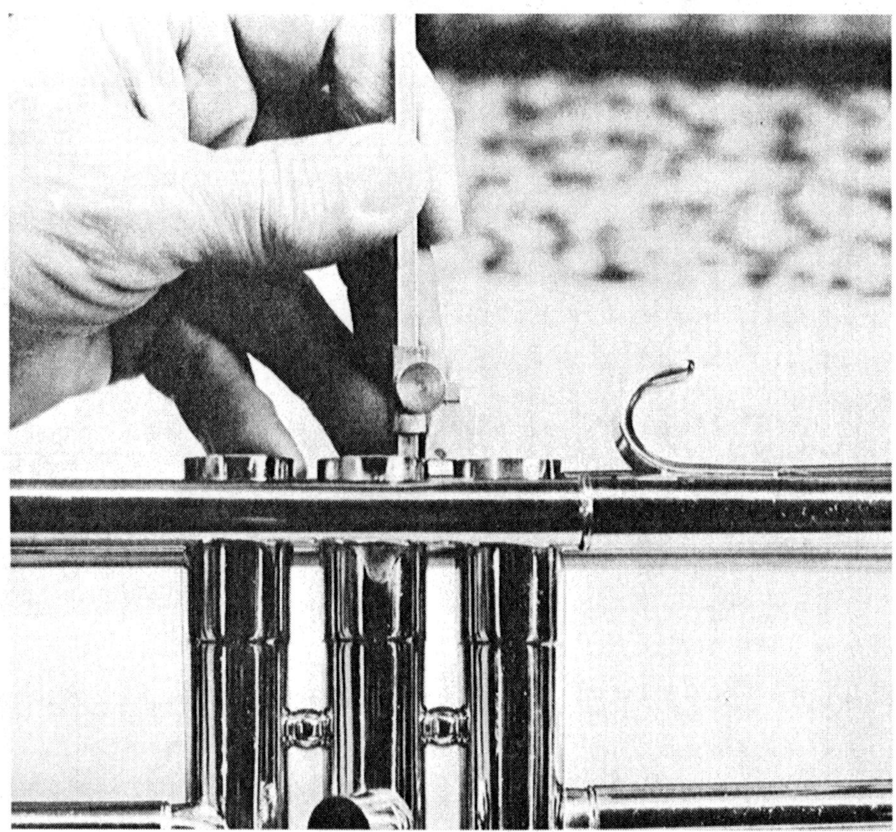

Photo 87. Measuring for Up-Stroke Alignment

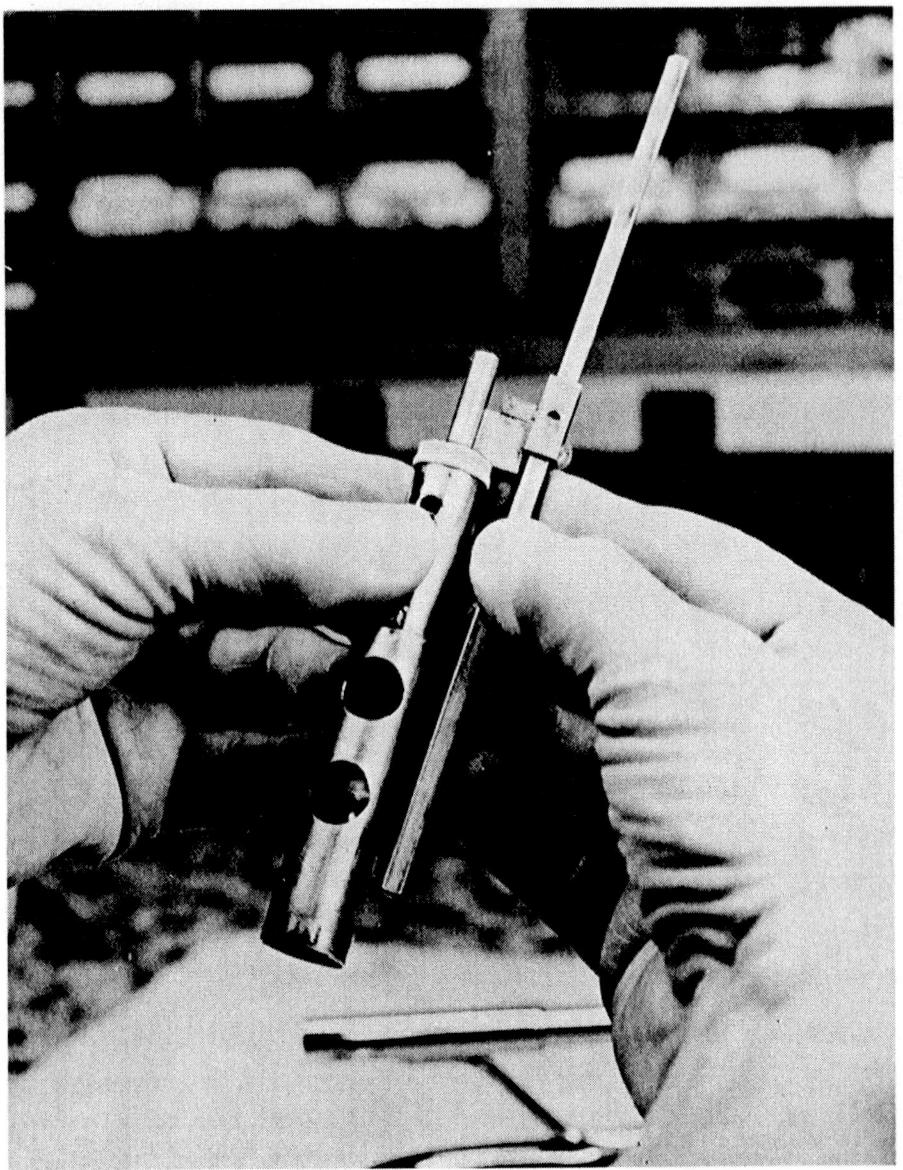

Photo 88. Transposing Measurement from Casing to Valve

The down-stroke, just as vital as the up-stroke, can be easily checked on a cornet or trumpet by removing the second valve slide, depressing the piston and checking by eye to see if the ports line up (Photos 89, 90, and 91). This regulation is made on newer horns with a felt or rubber washer in the groove in the top valve cap, and on older instruments with a combination of cork and felt washers in the finger button. When replacing finger button washers, be sure to put the washers on the valve stem, then screw on the finger button. If you place the washers in the finger button before putting it back on the stem there is the probability some material may come between the top of the stem and the button, causing a false regulation.

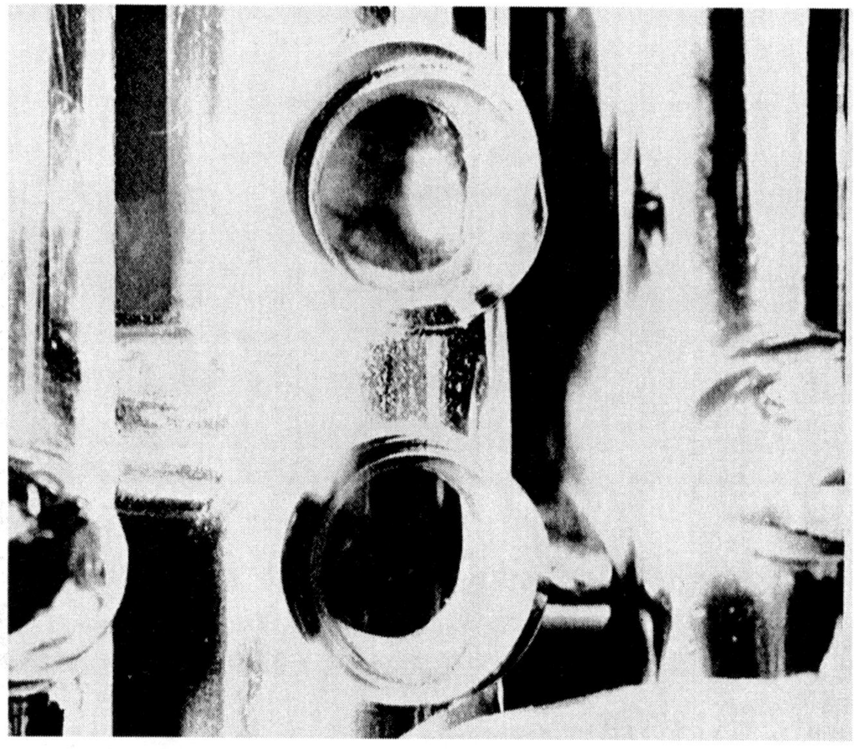

Photo 89. Finger Button Felt Too Thick

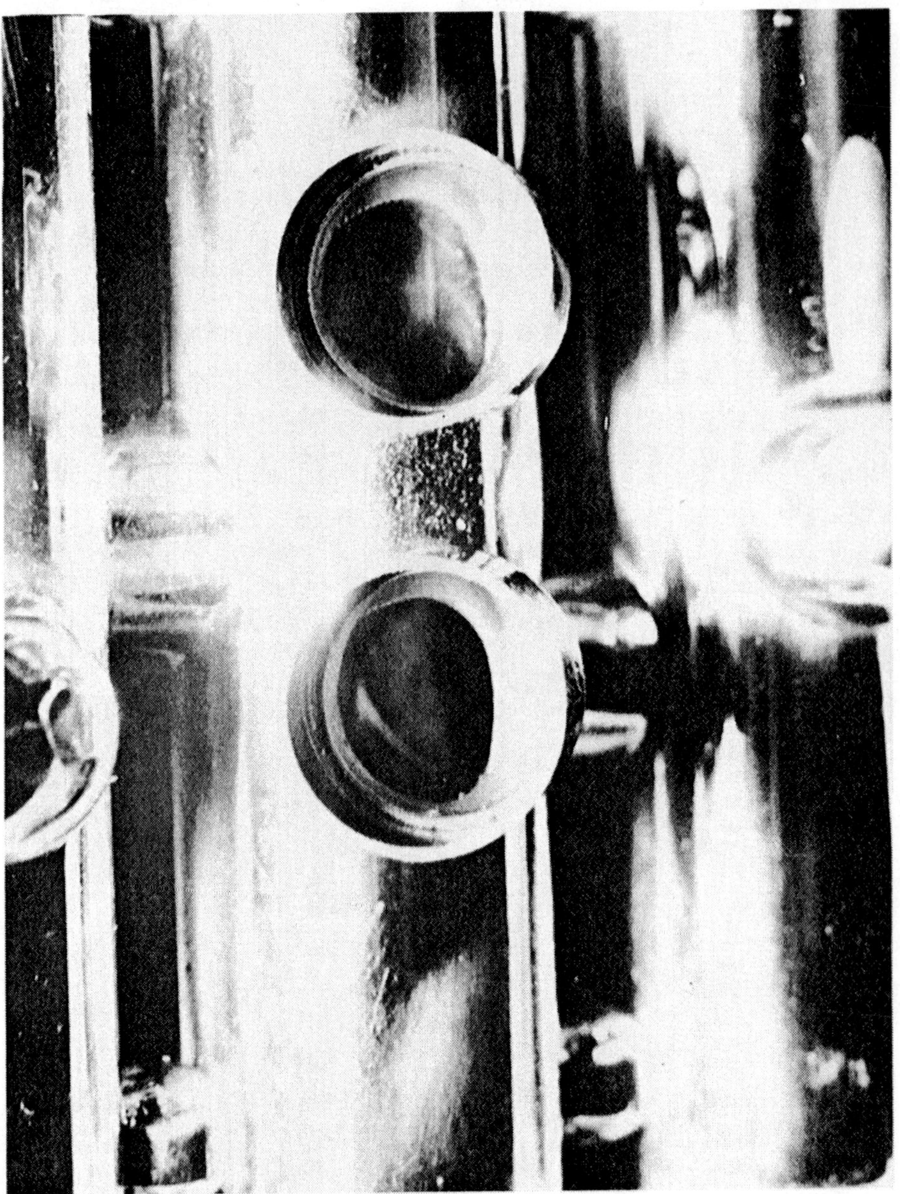

Photo 90. Finger Button Felt Too Thin

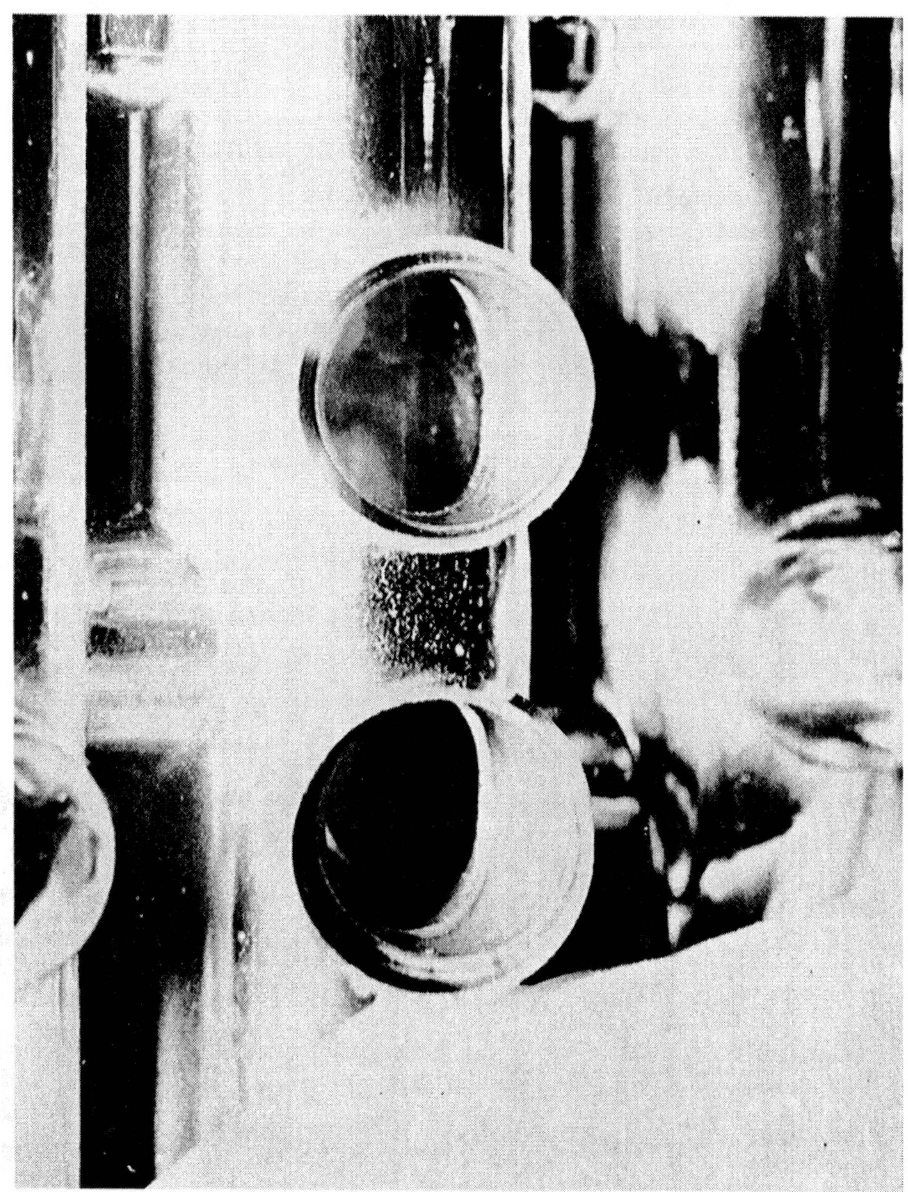

Photo 91. Finger Button Felt Correct–Ports Line Up.

Checking the down position on a baritone or bass where the second valve slide is bent around a corner making it impossible to see is a more difficult process and requires the use of a valve mirror and a flashlight or leak light. With the second valve in place, remove the first or third valve and caps depending on which casing is the easiest to look into. Insert the mirror from either top or bottom, light the mirror from the opposite end to make it possible to look into the casing and see through the connecting tube into the port in the second valve. Depress the valve and check the alignment by sight. The first and third valves take the same thickness of cork and felt as the second.

13

ROTARY VALVE BRASS

Keeping the inside of the French horn clean is vital. The bore of the mouthpipe, being of smaller diameter and greater length than the other brasses, should be given special attention and cleaned regularly. This is easier to do on some horns than on others, because if the mouthpipe runs into the valves without a removable slide in between, the valve should be removed at every cleaning to prevent pushing dirt into the valve proper, as the snake cleans the mouthpipe.

Due to the fact that rotary valves are not plated and very often not oiled, they will build up deposits from saliva, to the point where they work very reluctantly or not at all. To remove this accumulation, immerse the valve for a few seconds in a solution of muriatic acid and water, then wash the valve in detergent and water and polish it lightly with brass polish.

When the buildup inside the casing is severe, use Q-tips dipped in the acid solution to remove it. Never try to scrape or scour the buildup from either the valve or the casing, since you will surely cause serious and permanent damage. Now wash and flush the instrument carefully. A good repairman would give the entire horn an acid bath, then neutralize the acid with a cyanide rinse. You need not be concerned about failure to neutralize the small amount of acid that will get into the horn using the described Q-tip procedure if you wash and flush the horn as carefully as possible following the cleaning.

Those of you who have never removed a rotary valve should heed the following instructions. Remove the valve cap, then the string or mechanical lever from the valve. Now unscrew the screw that holds the stop arm ONE turn only, and tap straight down on the screw with a rawhide mallet while supporting the horn with your fingers directly underneath around the valve you are removing (Photo 92). Repeat this process, loosening the screw one turn only each time until the valve and back bearing are free. If you turn the screw out more than one turn at a time it is very easy to hit it a glancing blow and break it off. This usually means a trip to a repair shop to remove the broken screw.

When the valves and casings are clean, replace each valve in its proper casing and spin it with your fingers. If it fails to spin freely but appears to be clean, there is probably a burr on the stem or the bearing that should be removed by a repairman.

When replacing the back bearing, be sure to line up the mark on the edge of the bearing with the mark on the casing. If you find it necessary to tap the bearing into place, use only a small rawhide mallet and tap it very lightly all the way around so that you do not tilt the bearing on the valve stem. See that it is down tight to the casing all the way around. The valve will bind if the bearing is tilted.

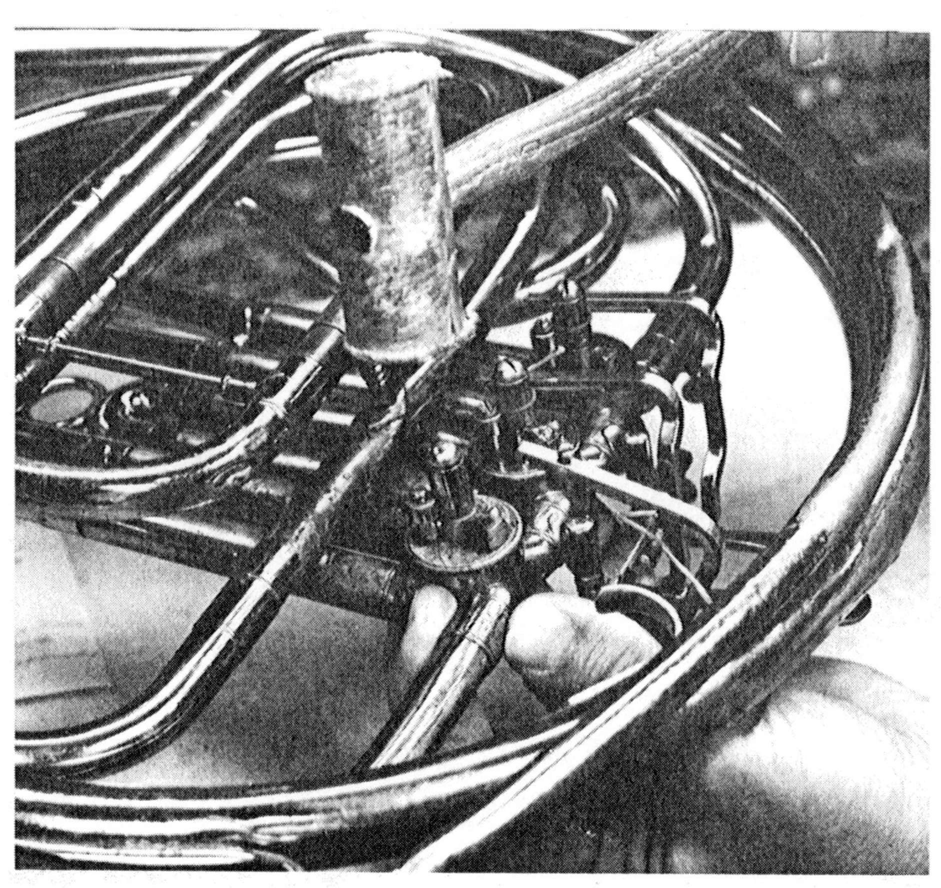

Photo 92. Removing Rotary Valve

Exact regulation is essential for good tone quality and response. Before replacing the valve cap, replace the stop arm and snug down the stop arm screw. Do not overtighten, since this screw breaks easily. Now check the alignment of the mark on the end of the valve stem with the marks on the back bearing as the stop arm contacts the cork stops on each end of its throw. If the mark on the valve stem goes past the mark on the bearing (as seen in Photo 93), remove the old cork and replace it with a new one. If it does not reach the mark (as seen in Photo 94), trim the cork stop, a thin slice at a time, or sand it until the marks align exactly. Be sure the mark on the edge of the bearing is aligned with the mark on the casing (Photo 95) or your cork regulation will be meaningless.

Most beginning teachers have difficulty re-stringing the valves. My advice is to get another horn that is strung correctly to copy, or else remove only one string at a time until you are familiar with the procedure. Buy 30 to 50 lb. test fish line with which to re-string your valves.

The trombone trigger valve is serviced exactly the same as a rotary French horn valve.

Never neglect an unsoldered or broken brace, because this will compound the stress on the other braces and surely will break others loose or bend some tubing. If you cannot resolder it yourself, take it to a shop as soon as possible. "A stitch in time saves nine" was seldom more appropriate.

Photo 93. Cork Stop Too Thin–Replace

Photo 94. Cork Stop Too Thick–Trim To Size

Photo 95. Back Bearing and Cork In Proper Alignment

Repair Notes

14

TROMBONE

With a relatively inexpensive set of straight trombone mandrels you can repair your own trombone slides. You will need a dent hammer and a large vise to hold the mandrel. Most schools have shops with vises already conveniently installed, and shop teachers who are usually glad to have you use their facilities. Some will even assist you with your projects.

Bent slides, slides out of parallel and dirty slides probably rank equally with dents as causes for poor slide action.

Keeping the trombone clean should be the responsibility of the student, but unless the teacher insists and inspects regularly, many students will neglect this. Having really nothing to do with the action of the slide, but of equal importance, is the cleanliness of the inside of the inner slide. If this is brushed and flushed regularly, there will never be a buildup here, and a trombone snake-type brush, detergent and water will keep it clean. If the horn has been neglected and corrosion has formed that will not brush out, take it to a repair shop for an acid bath. The slide should shine like a rifle barrel on the inside. In case you try to clean this with anything other than a trombone brush, use great care on the upper slide because of the venturi tube. This is a tube with a double taper soldered inside the inner slide at the mouthpiece end forming the mouthpiece receiver and a mouthpipe (Photo 96).

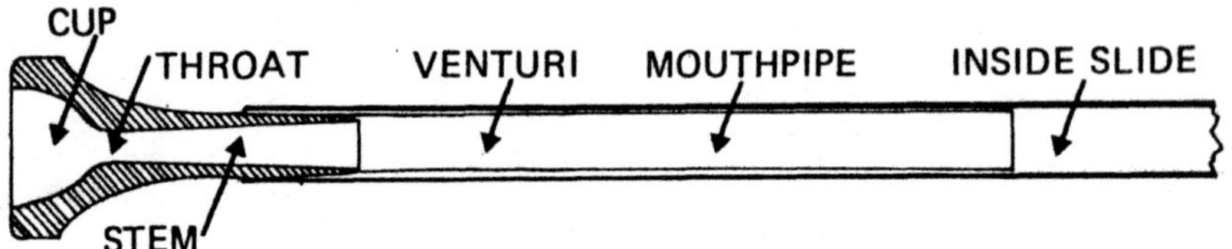

Photo 96. Cutaway of the Venturi Tube

It is about 8 inches long and narrows the diameter of the bore at this point. If you are unaware of this you might get a cloth stuck here, or damage the venturi with the cleaning rod since it is made of very thin brass.

When using the trombone cleaning rod, use a strip of cloth 4 to 8 inches wide (depending upon the thickness of the cloth and the bore of the instrument) and about a yard long. Insert a corner of the cloth into the eye of the rod, then bring the long cloth over the end of the rod and twist it down the entire length of the rod holding on to both cloth and rod as you clean. (See Photos 97-99).

From the standpoint of good slide action, it is the inside of the outer slide that must be kept clean (Photo 99A).

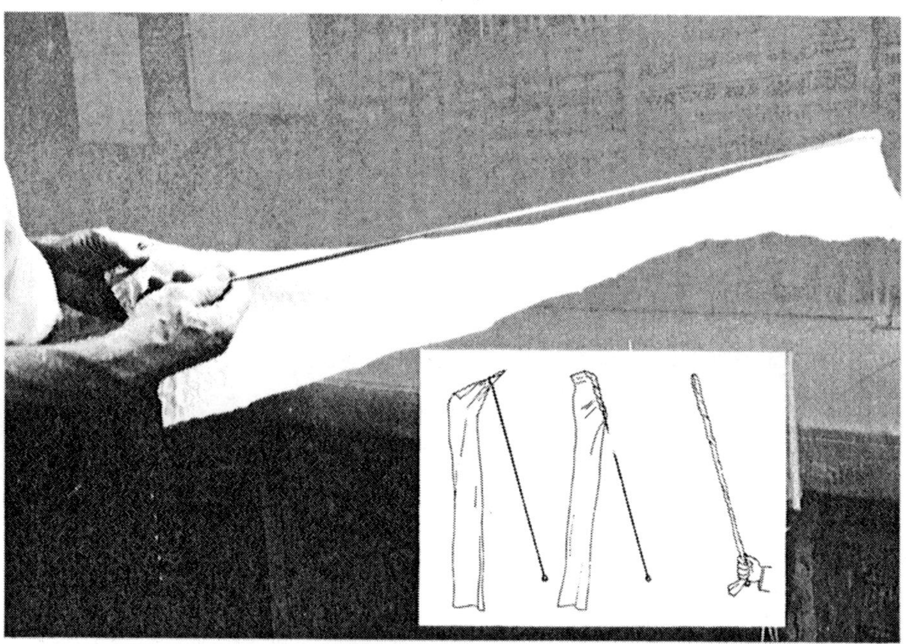

Photo 97. Corner of Cloth Through Rod Eye

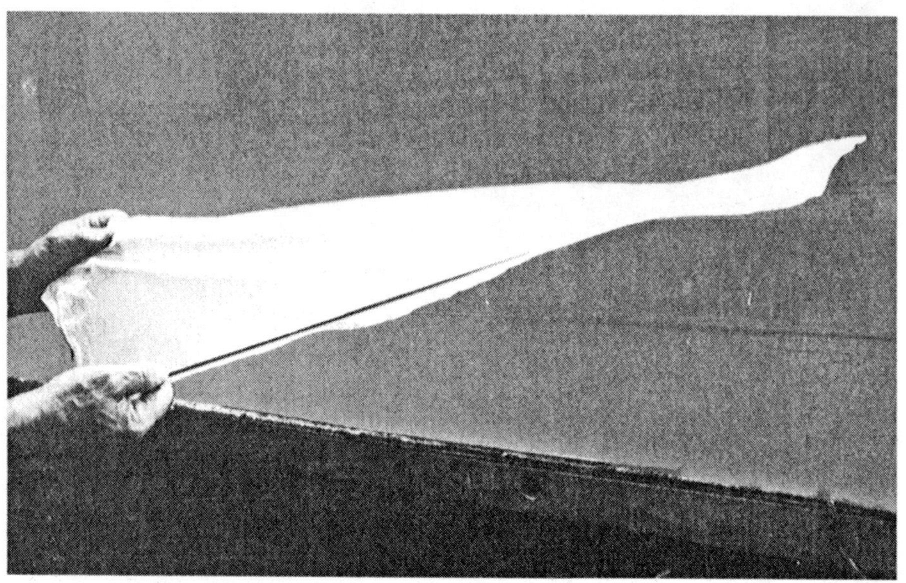

Photo 98. Cover Eye End with Cloth

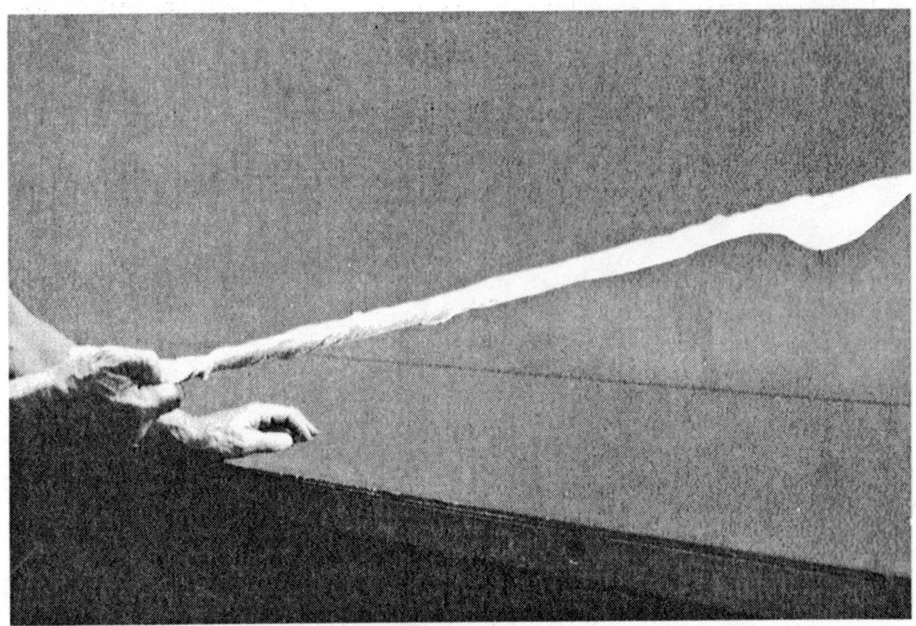

Photo 99. Twist Cloth Around Rod

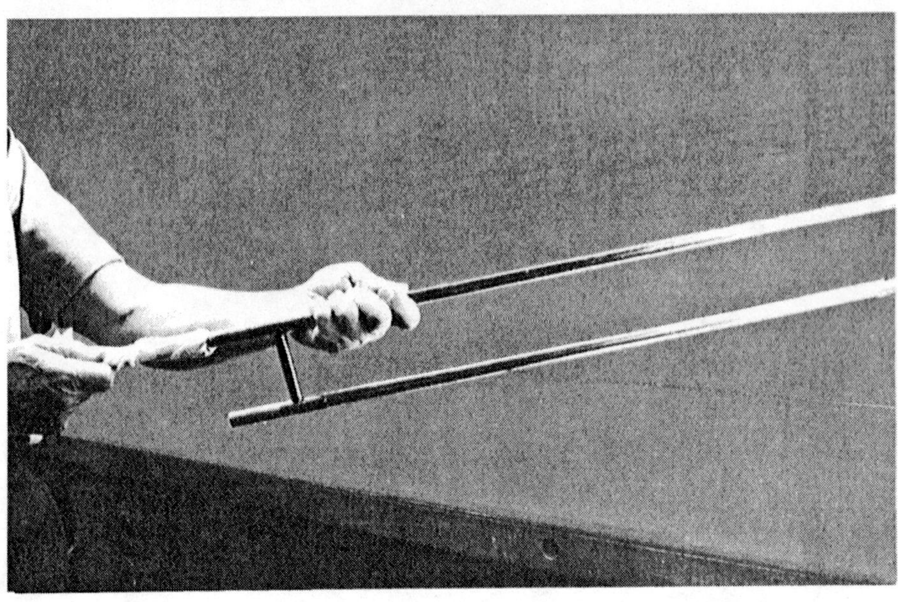

Photo 99A. Cleaning Slide with Cloth-Covered Rod

As with rotary valves, this slide is without plating and is susceptible to corrosion. If it is neglected, an acid bath in a repair shop is about the only way to restore it. With thorough regular cleaning no buildup will take place. Use the trombone snake-brush to keep the bow clean, and the cloth and rod to remove old cream or oil from the slide proper.

Let's assume that the slides are clean but you still get poor action. Find out whether it is the upper or lower slide or both that are binding by trying each one separately. As an example, the lower slide is free, but the upper slide binds in one or more places. Remember that with the exception of about 4 1/2-inches of the inner slide, called the stocking (which is that larger outside diameter on the end of the inner slides), there is very little contact between inner and outer slides. Therefore, if a dent is the cause of the problem you should get a pretty good idea of its location by noting where the stocking is when the binding occurs. Sometimes it is easier to locate a dent by feel than by sight.

Using the largest mandrel that will go into the slide, support the end of the mandrel in the vise, place the slide on it and raise the dent or dents with light, glancing blows of a well polished dent hammer as shown in Photo 100. We say "raise" the dent because it seems to be next to impossible to bring the dent back to level since the brass was stretched when the dent was made. To remove it, we must stretch it again between the mandrel and the hammer, raising a bump in place of the indentation.

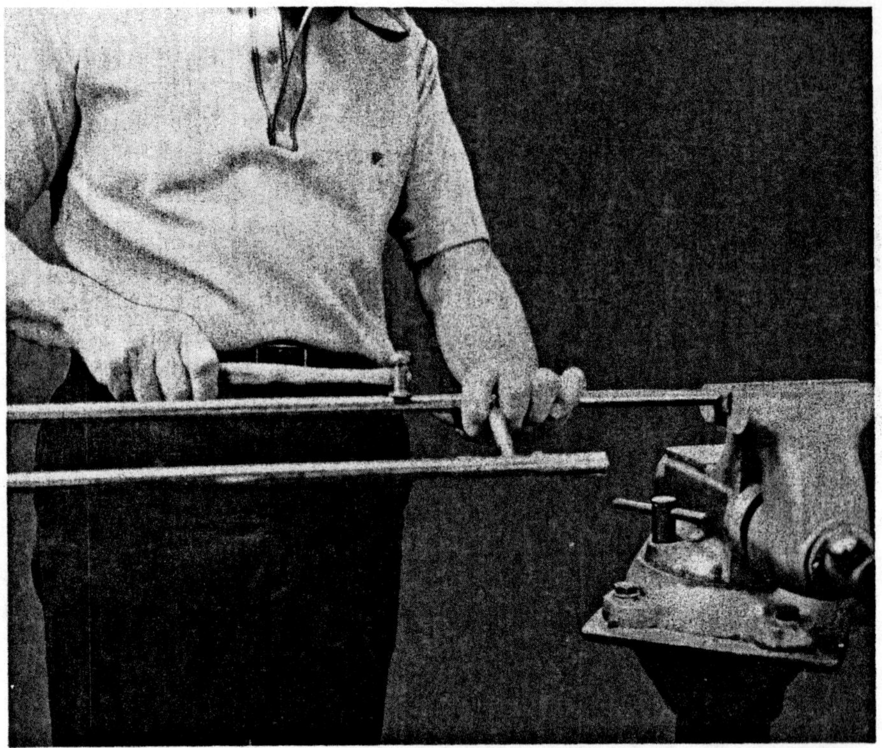

Photo 100. Removing Slide Dent

If the individual slide is still not free, and you are sure all dents are removed, you have a bent slide. Usually it is the outer slide that causes the problem. Sight down the slide as shown in Photo 101. If you can see the curve you can straighten it. If your eye cannot detect it, take it to a repair shop. A bent slide is straightened by stroking it using light pressure on the high side of the curve. Hold the open end in one hand and hang the bow end on the bench, or a corner of a piece of dowel supported in the vise (Photos 102 and 103). Always support the bow end of the side you are trying to straighten. Never support the lower side on the bench while working on the upper (Photo 104), as you will surely twist the slide.

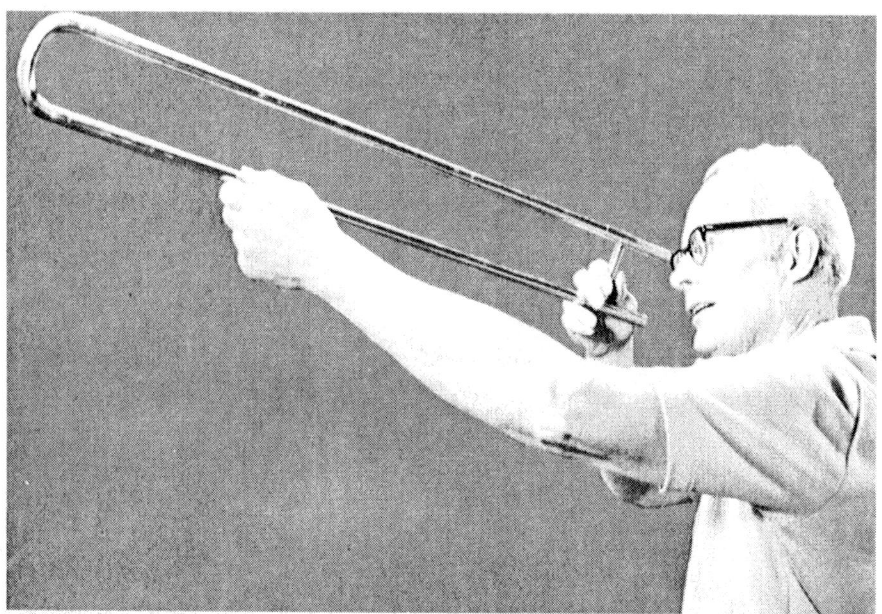

Photo 101. Sighting Slide to Detect Curve

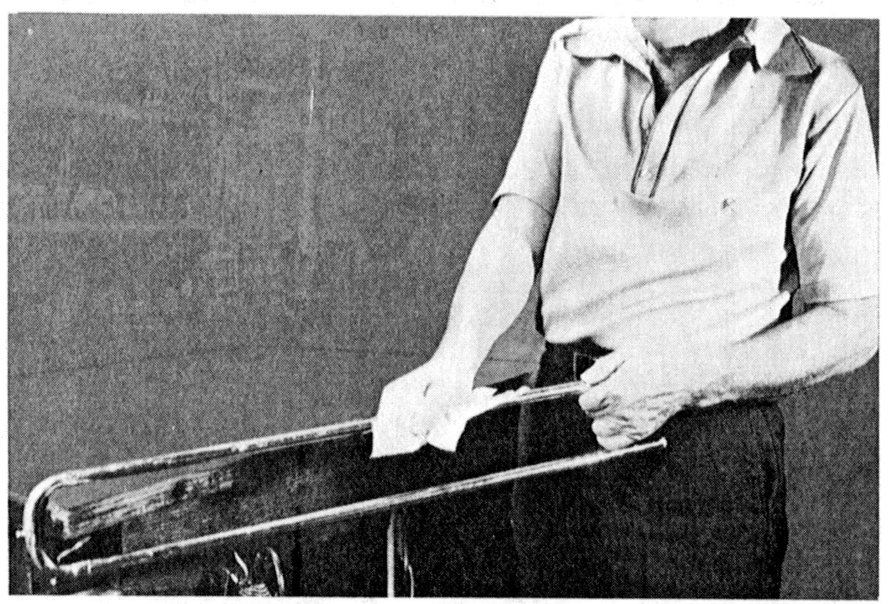

Photo 102. Placement of Slide When the Curve Is Up

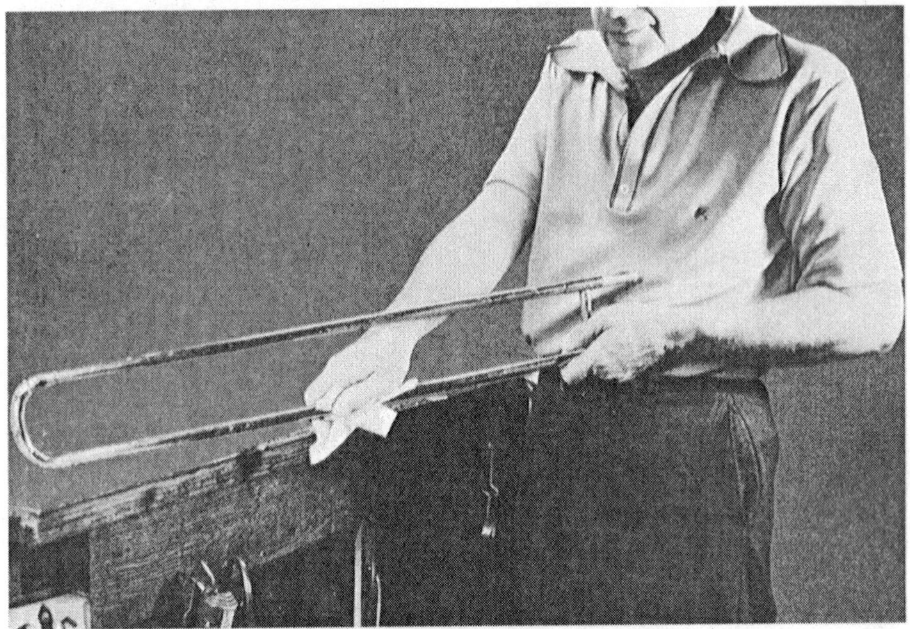

Photo 103. Placement of Slide When the Curve Is Down

Photo 104. NEVER Hold Slide This Way

Both upper and lower slides may work perfectly individually, but bind when assembled. One of two things might still be wrong. The slides may be out of parallel, or they may be twisted.

The inner slides have been sprung out of parallel if the stockings do not meet the corresponding outer slides exactly (Photo 105). Never, never, never take hold of the stocking end of the inner slides to try to bend them together or apart.

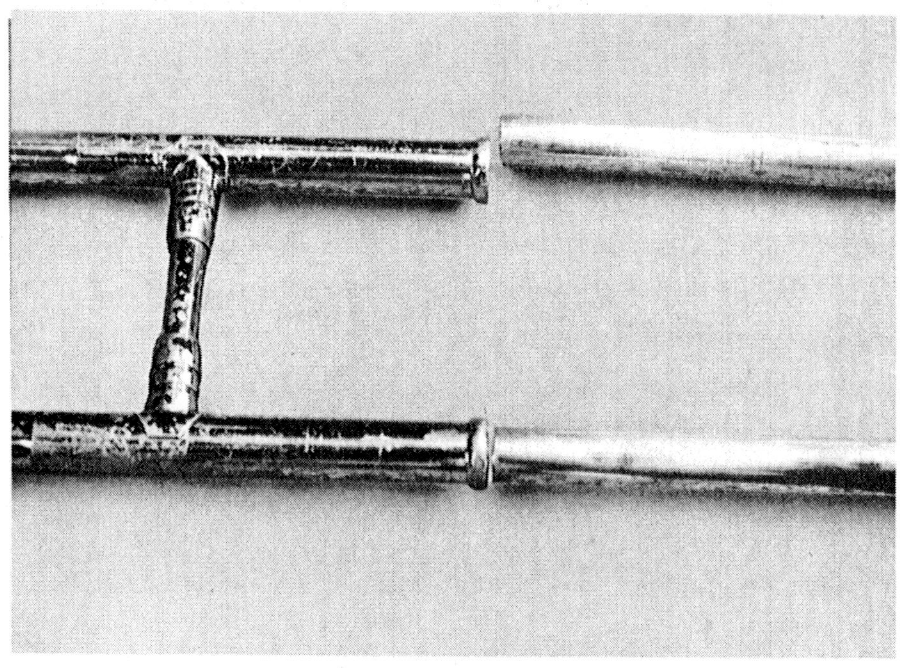

Photo 105. Inner Slide Sprung

Rather, give yourself a mechanical advantage by extending the braced end of the slide with a tapered punch, or better still, the mouthpiece in the upper slide and a dowel or brass rod extending from the lower (Photo 106). Now you can close or open the stocking end by applying opposite pressure on the braced end. This method will bend the brace slightly instead of putting a damaging curve in the slides.

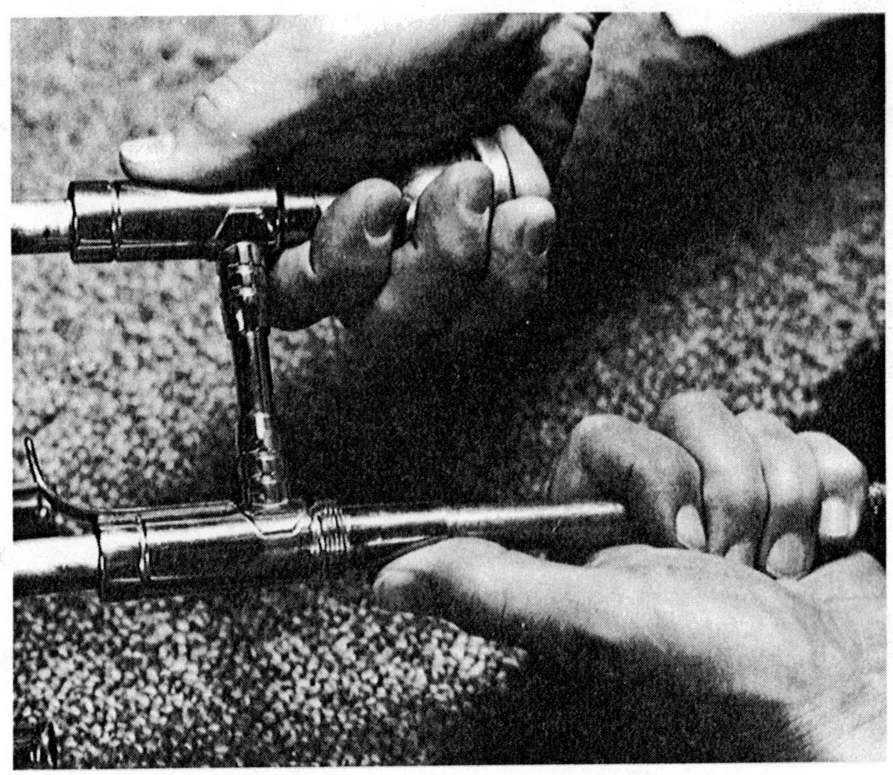

Photo 106. Aligning Sprung Inner Slide

To determine whether the slide has been twisted or not, lay the outer slide flat on as flat a surface as is available and tap each of the four corners with your finger. If a corner is high, it will move under your finger. Take the bow in one hand and the cross brace in the other and twist the high corner down as shown in Photo 107. Ideally your flat surface should be short enough to contact the straight part of the slide only, letting the bow ferrules and the brace reinforcement hang over on each end. Should you plan on doing a lot of this it is an easy job to cut a piece of plate glass 7 inches wide and 18 inches long to use as a leveling plate. You can purchase a metal or stone leveling plate, but they are quite expensive. Determine a twist in the inner slide in the same manner and remove it with the mechanical advantage as described earlier (Photo 108).

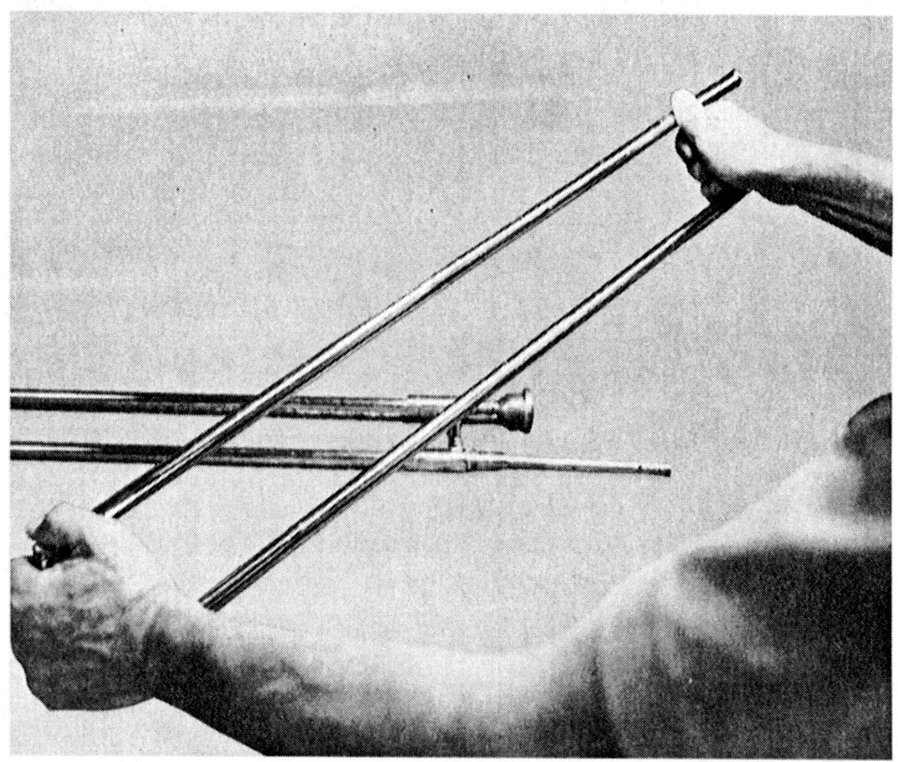

Photo 107. Removing Twist From Outer Slide

Photo 108. Removing Twist From Inner Slide

Keep the tuning slide clean and lubricated with STP and use a regular bottle brush to clèan the bell bore. To service the trigger valve, refer to Chapter 13, "Rotary Valve Brass."

I am strongly opposed to sending a trombone away to be buffed and relacquered because I have seen shops remove all the raised slide dents with emory and buffing so the slide looks and feels brand new, but so much brass is removed in the process that the first little "tunk" does major damage to the refinished slide. Remember the brass in these slides is only from about .006 to .011 thick to begin with.

15

SOLDERING

To continue to use an instrument with a brace flange or soldered connection of any kind that has broken loose is asking for trouble. One broken connection greatly increases the stress on the rest of the instrument and you could find yourself with major repair nècessary if you neglect the broken joint. No great amount of skill or investment in tools is necessary to make this repair.

There are two entirely different types of solder used on a brass instrument, soft solder and hard or silver solder. It is important to understand where each type is used. Hard solder is used on all the tube connections into the valve casings, and on all the brace rods or tubes to the brace flanges. The hard soldered joints are, for all practical purposes, a weld. The materials when joined are red hot and the metal actually fuses. Consequently, hard soldered joints are much stronger than soft soldered joints, and will not come apart when heat sufficient to melt soft solder is used on an adjacent area. All other connections are soft soldered–namely tubes connected with a ferrule and brace flanges to tubes or casings. For soft solder to hold, there must be a relatively large area of contact (Photo 109).

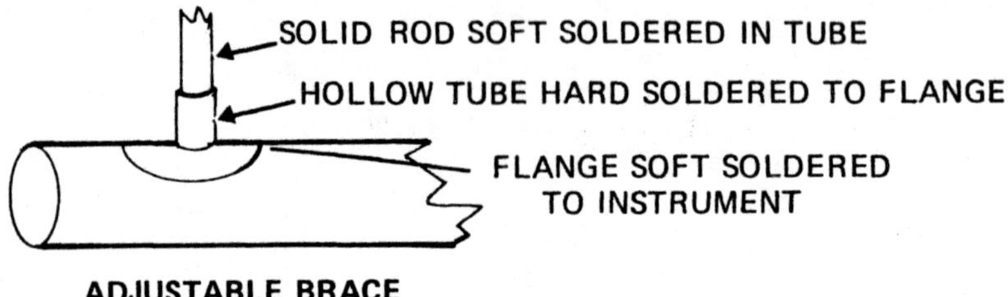

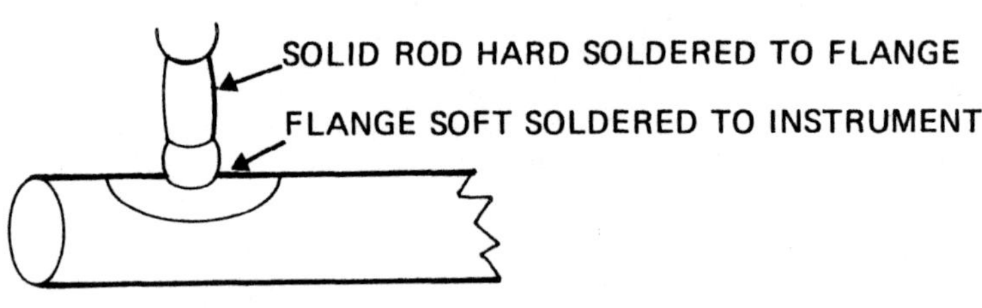

Photo 109. Soft and Hard Soldered Connections

A brace where the rod or hollow tube has broken away from the flange cannot be successfully repaired with soft solder as there simply is not enough area contact. To hard solder a broken brace it is necessary that the brace be completely removed from the instrument, every vestige of soft solder scraped away, hard soldered, cleaned, polished and resoldered to the horn. This is a time-consuming process and therefore costly; consequently, it is cheaper to install a new brace than to repair the old one. I mention this because so often horns come into my shop with a big glob of soft solder around the end of a broken brace rod where someone has tried to make the repair with soft solder. It never holds.

You need four things to make a soft solder repair. A torch, solid wire solder, flux and emery cloth. A propane torch such as most of you already own will do the job, but a smaller pin-point flame would be better. At best you will burn some lacquer around the joint, so the more confined you can keep the flame the better off you will be. Instrument repair supply houses sell a propane torch, smaller than the regular hardware store variety, that shoots a tiny, hot flame in a small concentrated area. For the solder itself, use solid wire solder either of a 50-50 or 40-60 proportion. Never use acid-core or resin-core solder on a brass instrument. Get your solder in as small a diameter wire as is available at your local hardware. 1/16-inch diameter is preferable to 1/8-inch if you can get it, since it is easy to get too much solder on the joint with the larger diameter. Any good soft solder flux such as Nokorode soldering paste or a liquid flux will satisfy. You will need a sheet of emery cloth which can be conveniently ripped into narrow strips.

Use a scraper, a file, steel wool or emery cloth, but no matter what you use, both pieces to be joined must be absolutely free from grease, oil or dirt of any kind. Even the natural oil or your skin from a touch of a fingertip may hinder good solder flow. The secret to good soldering is meticulous cleanliness.

Even though solder will fill in a pretty good sized void, the job will be stronger if you contour the parts to be joined so that they will fit as closely together as possible. With a small brush, Q-tip or pipe cleaner, coat both pieces with flux where you desire the solder to flow. Use a piece of soft iron binding wire or stovepipe wire, as we used to call it, to pull the joint together if necessary, or to hold the pieces in place if there is any chance of their slipping. Apply the tip of the flame to the heavier of the pieces to be joined, and play it around a bit to heat the pieces as evenly as possible and to burn as little of the adjacent lacquer as possible. Heat the pieces only as hot as necessary for the solder to flow. Most novices use too much heat and too much solder. When you are sure the joint is completely filled, keep just enough heat on it to enable you to wipe any excess solder from around the edge.

When the joint has cooled, file or scrape away any solder that still shows and any lacquer that has been burned. Polish the bare brass with 0000 steel wool and touch it up with lacquer. I find it easier to use a small brush and brushing lacquer than to try to mask the rest of the instrument enough to use lacquer from a spray can.

Hard soldering is more difficult, but not necessarily beyond your grasp. You will need a coil of hard solder, some hard solder flux, and unless you have access to a torch that uses oxygen in combination with acetylene or gas in some form, you will need several pieces of asbestos to form a reflection screen of some sort. With good reflection and heat retention you can hard solder with your propane torch.

Use hard solder to repair broken woodwind keys, sax key guards, etc., and any place where it is necessary to join brass or key silver end-to-end, or where the joining area is small. If you are working on a key guard, or anything with an area that was soft soldered to the horn, it is essential to remove every trace of soft solder before proceeding.

Clean and flux the parts to be joined and align them on an asbestos pad or fire brick. This alignment can sometimes prove to be the most difficult part of the job. To get the correct angle on a broken clarinet bridge key, for example, can be a bit tricky. Use pins and pieces of asbestos block to position the key and to reflect and hold the heat as confined as possible around the joint. Use a jig only if it is impossible to align the pieces properly on a block. The block helps to hold and reflect the heat, whereas the jig clamps act as heat sinks, drawing heat away from the key as well as making it difficult to set up a heat reflection screen. The key jig is expensive.

If the pieces you are joining are of different thicknesses, as when joining a brace rod to a flange, apply the flame to the heavier piece, otherwise you will burn a hole in the thin piece before the thick piece gets red. After applying the flux, apply the flame until both ends to be joined are red hot. Touch the hard solder to the joint and it should flow in and spread immediately. Let it cool, dunk in the muriatic acid and water solution to dissolve the hardened flux and wash. File or grind away any excess silver solder and polish, if desired.

Not too many of you are going to want to try your hand at hard soldering. In spite of this, it is good to know just what is involved in the process, and if you have the necessary information and materials on hand, you are in a position to make an emergency repair if the situation should arise.

Repair Notes

16

MISCELLANEOUS

An attempt has been made in the preceeding chapters to cover certain aspects of maintenance and repair on band instruments that I believe the regular instrumental music teacher and band instructor is capable of doing. Some of you could and would do much more if you had the time, and to some of you such work holds no interest or desire, so only a very minimum amount, if any, is attempted. The object of this effort on my part, as well as on yours, is to save a week, two weeks, a month, or even more when an instrument has to be tied up in a shop waiting its turn for repair. With a beginner especially, this "time off' may bring about such a loss of interest that the student drops out of your program.

Piccolo, oboe, bassoon, the low clarinets and saxophone have not been discussed for the simple reason that these instruments are difficult to regulate, and unless you have a greater-than-average interest, you should take them to a repair shop. There are, however, certain basics on each that you can handle, thus saving some time and money.

With the piccolo as with the flute, it is of utmost importance that the head joint cork be airtight and properly positioned. You should get a perfect vacuum on the head joint when covering the blow hole with your finger and sucking out the air. If you cannot get good suction here, replace the cork with a new one, or enlarge the old cork with Scotch Magic Tape. If you are positive the cork does not leak and the suction is still not good, the indication points to a leak in the soldering around the embouchure plate. When you check the positioning of the head joint cork, be sure to use a C piccolo rod on a C piccolo and a Db rod on the Db piccolo. A fraction of an inch in the positioning of this cork can make a big difference in the tonality.

I do not recommend that you attempt to replace any piccolo pads on either the right or left hand stacks, with the exception of the first finger, left hand, due to the delicate regulation involved. Unlike the flute, there are no regulating screws to assist you in the process. The regulation is achieved through the amount of cement under a pad or the bending of a lug. You can, however, replace the trill key pads, the B (first finger, left hand), and the low Eb, since all of these keys are independent. Thin bladder clarinet pads will usually work on the low Eb, but you should have regular piccolo pads, sizes 6 1/2 through 9, for the trill keys and the B. Luckily enough, these are the pads that often are the first to break their skins. Invest in a plastic oil can with a hypodermic needle applicator and make sure the instrument has a tiny drop of oil at least twice a year in every working slot. If you use the piccolo for night football games, oil it every two weeks during football season. Insist that the student swab it clean following every session.

Because I consider it of such great importance, I repeat what I have mentioned earlier in Chapter 2 on woodwind instrument body care concerning the use of a feather as an oboe swab. Take great care in making your cloth oboe swabs. Two are necessary, one very narrow strip for the upper joint and a slightly wider strip for the lower joint. I strongly advise against using the oboe in your marching band. Every fall I pin cracked oboes that were used out of doors at night. It is far more satisfying to the student, the rest of the band, to you and to the listening audience to hear an extra saxophone or two in the football band in place of the oboe.

There are a few keys on the oboe that have no connection or regulation with any other keys. These pads you can replace if you have pads of the correct thickness. I do not recommend your replacing any of the stack key pads, or even the little finger key pads on the lower joint. If none of the pad skins are broken and you still have leaks, the problem is either a bent key or faulty regulation. Unless you are very good at figuring out what does what and why, don't try to do any oboe regulating. Take it to a repair shop. Check your oboes frequently for signs of a crack, and get them pinned as soon as they appear. You can clean and fill a crack with lacquer or clear fingernail polish which will stop the leak temporarily, but this will do nothing to discourage further progress of the crack. Keep the mechanism oiled.

The bassoon does not present the regulation problem existing in the piccolo, oboe or saxophone. In fact, most of the keys are relatively independent of each other. There are, however, so many other factors peculiar to the bassoon that I do not recommend your trying to do any major repair on it. If your problem is a pad with a broken leather, you can probably replace it satisfactorily assuming you have the correct size and thickness pad on hand. Seldom, however, is the problem that simple. Chipped tone holes, leaks around posts, binding action or play in the action, poor seating on the pads, boot gasket or boot cap leaks, etc., all tend to make the bassoon quite unique and usually no job for a novice. See to it that the bocal is kept clean and the key mechanism oiled. Pay careful attention to proper instruction in assembling. I recommend having a joint lock installed if your bassoon is not so equipped. The use of a seat strap in combination with a neck strap and a proper crutch are essential to good playing habits.

One would tend to assume that if you keep your soprano clarinets in good playing condition you can do the same with your altos, basses and contras. There are two reasons why this assumption is incorrect. First, the cost of keeping the necessary inventory of pads on hand for two bassoons and a half-dozen low clarinets is prohibitive, and second, there is a good deal of stack regulation involved with the closed hole mechanism that does not exist on the soprano clarinet. The regulation of a contra-bass clarinet that has been only slightly misused can be very frustrating. Stress the importance of keeping these instruments clean and dry with regular swabbing, and oil the mechanism twice a year. As with your oboes, do not use these low clarinets at night footbal games if they have wooden bodies. It is next to impossible to swab the Leblanc contra clarinets, and really not necessary if the goose neck and tuning crook are dried every time and washed at frequent intervals.

Due to the slanted playing position of the saxophone, the three left hand palm keys, high F, Eb, and D, get a great deal of saliva, causing them to harden and crack open long before any of the other pads deteriorate, except for the low Eb. I think it would pay you to buy sax pads in sizes 21/32, 22/32, 23/32, and 24/32-inch with which to replace these. By using a fairly generous amount of shellac or pad cement you will be able to shift these pads with your pad slick in exactly the same manner in which you shift the four lower pads on a soprano clarinet in order to seal the tone holes.

As with the low clarinets, the cost of keeping an adequate supply of saxophone pads on hand is prohibitive. Furthermore, it is usually not so much a broken pad leather that is the problem, but a bent key causing a leak or missing corks or compressed felts fouling up the regulation. Consequently, unless you are willing to spend a great deal of time learning how to regulate a saxophone and straighten bent pad cups, I recommend taking the instrument to a repair shop.

Your job regarding the saxophone is to insist on proper swabbing, keeping the mechanism oiled and the neck and mouthpiece washed clean. Once every week, remove the neck octave key and clean the neck with a sax neck brush, warm water and detergent. You wouldn't believe how filthy the inside of a saxophone gets that is not swabbed regularly—or would you? Check your students' instruments and see for yourself.

Repair Notes

INDEX

References to drawings are printed in boldface type. Numbers in italics refer to the photographic inserts; the first number(s) is that of the location of the insert, the second that of the page in the insert.

A

B

C

T

V

W